Totally Chill: My Complete Guide to Staying Cool

A Stress Management Workbook for Kids With Social, Emotional, or Sensory Sensitivities

Christopher Lynch, PhD

Foreword by Kathy Selvaggi-Faden, MD

AAPC PUBLISHING

P.O. Box 23173
Shawnee Mission, Kansas 66283-0173
www.aapcpublishing.net

PUBLISHING

©2012 AAPC Publishing
P.O. Box 23173
Shawnee Mission, Kansas 66283-0173
www.aapcpublishing.net

Publisher's Cataloging-in-Publication

Lynch, Christopher, 1965-

    Totally chill: my complete guide to staying cool : a stress management workbook for kids with social, emotional, or sensory sensitivities / Christopher Lynch ; foreword by Kathy Selvaggi-Faden. -- Shawnee Mission, Kan. : AAPC Publishing, c2012.

    p. ; cm.

    ISBN: 978-1-937473-04-4
    LCCN: 2012933936
    Includes bibliographical references.
    Audience: Ages 8-13.
    Summary: Workbook to help students cope with and develop ways to prevent stress and anxiety. Topics include relaxation, flexible thinking, problem solving, getting organized, being healthy, getting along with other kids and using strengths and talents.

    1. Stress management for children--Juvenile literature. 2. Sensory integration dysfunction in children--Treatment--Juvenile literature. 3. Senses and sensation in children--Juvenile literature. 4. Social skills in children--Juvenile literature. 5. Relaxation--Technique--Juvenile literature. 6. Adaptability (Psychology) in children--Juvenile literature. 7. Problem solving in children--Juvenile literature. 8. [Stress management. 9. Senses and sensation. 10. Relaxation. 11. Problem solving. 12. Social skills.] I. Title.

BF723.S75 L96 2012
155.4/189042--dc23   1204

This book is designed in ITC Stone Sans and Bermuda Solid.
Cover Art: Penguin – © Lee Daniels, istockphoto; Ice: © archetype, Shutterstock
Interior Art: © Memo Angeles, Shutterstock; Ice: © archetype, Shutterstock
Printed in the United States of America.

Table of Contents

Dedication

For My Three Sons

☙ ☙ ☙ ☙ ☙

Acknowledgments

The children that I work with have been the source of inspiration for this book. Their intelligence, wit, and enthusiasm truly make it easy for me to come to "work" each day. For that I am eternally grateful. Sincere appreciation and admiration is also owed to the parents that I work with. Their care and drive to effect change have improved the quality of life for all children who face challenges.

I would like to gratefully acknowledge Dr. Walter Rosenfeld and Teri Criscione of Goryeb Children's Hospital for allowing me the freedom to develop the types of clinical programs that help to address the needs expressed in this book. Also from Goryeb Children's Hospital, I would like to acknowledge the Child Development Center and the Department of Pediatric Neurology for their endless enthusiasm and support.

I would like to thank Kirsten McBride and her editorial team at AAPC Publishing for their astute insights and recommendations. Special thanks and admiration goes to Virginia Biddulph for her assistance and dedication during the latter stages of the publication process. I would also like to thank all who reviewed my manuscript, including Harvey Bennett, MD, Kathy Selvaggi-Fadden, MD, Tosan Livingstone, MD, Janet Oberman, PhD, Carolyn Hayer of the New Jersey Statewide Parent Advocacy Network, and Martha Brecher, education advocate. Particular thanks to Margaret Hefferle of New Jersey Special Child Health Services for assisting with the review process as well as for her tireless devotion to helping families in need.

Finally, I would like to thank my family. Heartfelt gratitude to my wife, Angela, for her enthusiastic promotion of the book even before it was half finished, and special thanks to my children, Kieran, Liam, and Cáel, for being understanding when daddy goes to work to see "his kids."

FOREWORD

Throughout this book, I can hear Chris Lynch calmly challenging children to face their fears and develop less rigid/more flexible thinking.

I have known Chris for over 20 years and during that time have had the privilege of watching an excellent clinician at work. He has always been a thoughtful and thorough psychologist in the clinical situation. During his career Chris worked in Ireland for five years, developing a national reputation for himself and his work with individuals with Asperger Syndrome. On returning to the United States, he has built a practice of individual and group therapy that emphasizes practical coping strategies. His clinical program, AS-PIRATIONS, not only works on social skills that so many children need but also that critical piece involving social anxiety. He understands the children with whom he interacts in an uncanny way and can engage them in fun, practical solutions for coping with their situations.

Totally Chill: My Complete Guide to Staying Cool is filled with practical and kid-friendly exercises that I've seen work. For example, factual explanations about the body's reaction to stress help the reader to understand why relaxation techniques can work to conquer fears. Chris also identifies coping strategies that use visual learning techniques to cater to most children's needs.

Friendship circles, sensory sensitivities, bullying, and even an exercise on how to create your own school are topics that are recognized by every child. The book can be read independently by a child, but the adult can learn tips as well.

Enjoy the penguin and earn those ice blocks to make your strong igloo!

– *Kathleen Selvaggi Fadden, MD, medical director, Child Development Center, Goryeb Children's Hospital*

Introduction for Parents, Teachers, and Therapists

Totally Chill: My Complete Guide to Staying Cool

This book is designed for the child who has social, emotional, and/or sensory sensitivities. In parenting, teaching, and working with such kids, we often emphasize the learning of skills. This is only natural. We want our children, our students, and our clients to learn the skills that will help them to reach their potential in life. Some of the skill areas that we spend countless hours working on include social skills, fine- and gross-motor skills, skills to enhance sensory integration, language skills, and academic skills.

All of these skills are valuable and necessary, but stress management skills are often sorely missing from the list of things we teach to our kids. This is unfortunate given the wide range of problems that stress can cause. Stress can create challenges for learning and daily living. Stress also creates distress and can lead to meltdowns and behavioral outbursts.

The problem for children with sensitivities is twofold:

1. They are often vulnerable to multiple sources of stress due to their sensitivities.

2. They often lack the emotional resources to cope with this stress.

Children with sensitivities may consider as stressful a range of situations that for many other kids would not be a problem. Examples of situations that may be stressful for the sensitive child include:

- *A child who is a very fussy eater is forced to sit next to someone eating raw octopus*

- *A child who is sensitive to noise is reading quietly in the library when suddenly the fire alarm goes off*

- *A child who is a master at recalling facts is given a test that asks for his opinion*

- *A child who has difficulty making friends is rushed into a room full of kids she doesn't know*

- *A child is asked to come downstairs immediately while he is in the middle of counting up points from his collection of fantasy-game playing cards*

- *A child who is used to going to school via the same route every day must unexpectedly change her route due to road works*

- *A student who is reciting facts about ancient Roman battles is asked by the teacher to change the topic*

Any one of these situations may result in significant stress and anxiety for a highly sensitive child. Parents, teachers, and therapists often spend a significant amount of their own energy on trying to address these difficulties. In fact, trying to ease stress and anxiety may take up more time and energy than anything else they do. Consider the amount of time spent on reassuring and redirecting a child when he or she is in "panic mode." In addition, consider the amount of energy spent on trying to prevent stressful situations from occurring in the first place, or on trying to prepare the sensitive child for situations that cannot be prevented.

Who This Book Is For

This book is intended for children who have some type of inborn sensitivity. Sensitivities may be emotional, sensory, or social in nature. With regard to age, the book is intended for children ages 8 to 13 (grades 3 through middle school), but this may vary depending upon the child's level of conceptual understanding. The child may have an identifiable condition with a diagnosis (for example, autism spectrum disorder, bipolar disorder, attention deficit-hyperactivity disorder [ADHD], and anxiety disorders), or he or she may not.

Despite the differences that children with sensitivities may have, they tend to share a number of characteristics that make them prone to stress and anxiety. Some of these characteristics include:

@ Inflexible thought processing (everything is either black or white)

@ Difficulty with regulating sensory input (sound, light, tastes, etc.)

@ Social awkwardness (difficulties reading social cues, poor eye contact, etc.)

@ Overall high intelligence but much better at memorizing facts than understanding concepts

@ Difficulty with managing frustration (experiencing meltdowns when overwhelmed)

@ High levels of anxiety

@ A strong need for structure and routine

@ Tendencies to "fixate" on particular topics of interest

@ Poor "executive function" skills (organizing, planning, and adjusting to transitions)

The Purpose of This Book

As parents, teachers, and therapists you play an important role in helping children to manage stress. However, it is crucial that children develop skills to help them to manage their own stress *as independently as possible*. Despite all of our planning and programming, we cannot prevent children from encountering stressful situations. In addition, there will not always be a supportive person nearby who is able to jump in and resolve a stressful situation. Therefore, it is vital that the child learn and practice stress management skills that he or she can use when called for. This doesn't replace your important role. Instead, it adds to the child's growth and independence.

The goal of increasing independence for kids with sensitivities has shaped the format of this book. This workbook is meant to be read, completed, and used as much as possible by children. Your children, students, or clients should feel that this is "their" book. Certainly, some assistance may be called for in understanding and completing the chapters. However, the emphasis is always on the child's individual experience and the development of strategies that will work based on how he or she feels. The degree to which you will need to be involved depends upon your specific circumstances. Some general guidelines are as follows.

Parents

The degree to which you will need to assist your child depends upon such factors as the child's age, level of conceptual understanding, and motivation. Kids with sensitivities are often well aware of their stress and anxieties. Fortunately, they are also very motivated to learn and apply strategies *if they believe it will make them feel better.*

To help with understanding and motivation, the stress management principles in this book are presented in factual/scientific terms. I find that this makes learning more appealing for kids with sensitivities (since they tend to prefer concrete, factually based knowledge). If your child seems to be struggling with some of the concepts or assignments and is willing to let you assist, by all means do so. If your child can complete the book independently, it may still be beneficial for you to go over the material, provided that he or she is willing to share (I suggest gently encouraging this). This way you can prompt and remind your child to use the strategies that he or she has learned. If your child is unwilling to complete the book, don't force him or her to. In such cases, it may be best to allow your child to come to the material when he or she is ready.

To further help with motivation, the book is set up so that the child will earn two ice blocks at the end of each chapter. These ice blocks are used to build a stress management igloo. Your child will see the progress made on the igloo at the end of each chapter. An igloo is a strong structure that can help someone withstand the elements. Your child's stress management igloo will help him or her to withstand sources of stress that inevitably come up in life. At the end of the book, the child receives a certificate that includes a complete igloo that he or she can color or design. Your child may want to post this certificate in a place where it can serve as a reminder to use the tools he or she has learned.

Teachers

It is my belief that stress management should be taught in all schools to all kids (whether or not they have sensitivities). If you are teaching in self-contained classes or special schools, you may be able to incorporate the book into your curriculum. Members of your school's multidisciplinary team may also be willing and able to become involved. If you are teaching general education classes, you can still teach many of the principles of the book to all of your students. However, you may need to adjust references to issues that are directly relevant for the child with emotional, social, or sensory sensitivities.

Therapists

This book can easily be used as a template for group or individual therapy sessions. I devote a significant portion of the groups that I run for kids to completing the book. The speed with which you complete chapters will vary depending upon your clients' age and level of conceptual understanding. As noted above, the book is intended for children ages 8 through 13, but this general age range may be extended in particular circumstances. While it may be permissible to change the order of the presentation, I highly recommend completing Chapters 1 through 4 first, in order, as they set the stage for understanding stress management and lay down some of the fundamental strategies.

Chapter Summaries

Chapter 1: What Makes Me Stressed?

This chapter helps the reader to understand what stress is and how it relates to having some type of sensitivity. Throughout the book, emphasis is given to the idea that children have strengths as well as areas of need. The areas of need introduced in this chapter include rigid thought patterns, social skills difficulties, sensory sensitivities, school-related concerns, and having different talents and interests.

Chapter 2: The Science of Stress

This chapter explains stress from a scientific perspective. I find that kids with sensitivities find such explanations appealing and motivating. Six crucial concepts are covered: 1. Stress is something that has a real effect on mind and body. 2. Stress can happen from any change, whether good or bad. 3. Stress can arise from both real and imagined events. 4. Some stress is beneficial. 5. Too much stress can be detrimental. And 6. Stress can be managed.

Chapter 3: Relaxation Part 1: Relaxing My Body

In this and the following chapter, relaxation training is broken up into two parts. Chapter 3 emphasizes learning how to relax by addressing the body's physical reaction to stress. Particular attention is devoted to breathing and muscle relaxation strategies.

Chapter 4: Relaxation Part 2: Relaxing My Mind

In this second part of relaxation training, the reader learns how to relax through mental strategies. Particular attention is devoted to the use of imagery and meditation.

Chapter 5: Flexible Thinking

Rigid thinking, especially in relation to stress, is a hallmark characteristic of kids who have sensitivities. In this chapter, the reader learns how to identify when he or she is thinking too rigidly. The reader then learns to apply more adaptive and flexible ways of evaluating and responding to stressful situations.

Chapter 6: Problem Solving

This chapter teaches a method for evaluating and solving problems effectively. Specifically, a system for breaking down problem solving into concrete and manageable components is taught. To heighten motivation and understanding, the problem-solving strategies presented in this book are methodical and make use of visual supports.

Chapter 7: Getting Organized

Many kids who have sensory, emotional, or social sensitivities also have difficulty with executive function skills. These are the skills required for planning, prioritizing, and organizing. Such skills are addressed in this chapter. The chapter is broken down into three areas that are impacted by executive function: organizing belongings, learning how to prioritize, and time management.

Chapter 8: Being Healthy

Being healthy helps us to withstand stress better, both physically and mentally. Healthy habits are emphasized in this chapter. Four important areas are covered: eating habits, exercise, sleep, and physical health.

Chapter 9: Getting Along With Other Kids

Several socially related issues often result in stress for kids. Although this isn't a social skills book, this chapter provides guidance in three socially related areas: meeting new people, making friends, and dealing with bullies.

Chapter 10: Using My Strengths

The final chapter helps to highlight the different areas of strength that children can draw from in times of stress. This includes relishing one's talents, getting support from other people, and finding strength in one's belief system.

All kids (and all people!) have to deal with stress. Homework, making friends, getting along with a brother or sister, doing well at sports or a hobby, and taking tests are just some of the things that can make kids feel stressed out. However, some kids get stressed out quicker than others. Many of these kids have sensitive nervous systems. They may get upset quicker than other kids, get upset for more reasons than other kids, and have a harder time calming themselves back down after they get upset.

Perhaps you are a kid who has a sensitive nervous system. If you think you are, don't worry! There are a lot of good things about having sensitivities. Kids with sensitivities are smart, talented, caring, and have a good sense of humor. Even if you don't think you have sensitivities, this book may still offer you some helpful ideas.

You may be completing this book on your own. If so, please remember that this book is for kids of different ages. So, some of the words or information may be hard to understand. Don't be afraid to ask somebody for help if needed.

Throughout the book there are exercises for you to do to help with learning. This is YOUR book. So answer exactly the way that you feel.

At the end of each chapter, you will earn two ice blocks. These will be used to build your Stress Management Igloo. An igloo is a strong house made of ice. It can keep you protected from harm. Stress management skills also help you to be stronger and can help protect you from many different kinds of problems.

A kid who has sensitivities is like any other kid in many, many ways. But there are some things about being sensitive that can be really stressful. Five of these things include:

1. ONE-TRACK thinking

2. Difficulty with making FRIENDS

3. Overloaded SENSES

4. Problems at SCHOOL

5. Having different TALENTS and INTERESTS

Let's look at each of these areas.

ONE-TRACK Thinking

Kids with sensitivities are REALLY, REALLY GOOD at focusing on things that are interesting to them. They do well when things go the way that they want them to, and they are very good at doing things the same way all the time. In other words, they are very good at "One-Track Thinking."

Let's look at what YOU do well. (Write your answers in the blank spaces below.)

I am REALLY, REALLY GOOD at focusing on: _____.

I have a special talent for: _____.

I can talk to you all day long about: _____.

The one thing I can do the same way, every day is: _____.

I know many facts about: _____.

These are all special talents of yours and can be quite useful at times. However, there are some times when One-Track Thinking doesn't work so well.

One-Track Thinking doesn't work so well when:

@ You have to do more than one thing at once.

@ You have to stop doing what YOU want to do and do something that *someone else* wants you to do.

@ You cannot talk about what YOU want to talk about.

@ When the answer to something isn't clear or exact.

@ When you have to do something a different way than you are used to.

@ When your daily schedule changes without warning.

QUESTION: Why are these things mentioned in a book about stress?

ANSWER: Because sensitive kids usually find these things to be INCREDIBLY stressful!!! And things like this may happen to them EVERY SINGLE DAY!

EVERY DAY (or almost every day)

@ You have to do more than one thing at once.

@ You have to stop doing what *you* want to do and do something that *someone else* wants you to do.

@ You cannot talk about what YOU want to talk about.

@ You are asked questions that can't be answered with facts.

@ You have to do something in a different way than you are used to.

@ Your daily schedule will change (in some way) without warning.

These are things that happen to all kids (and adults). But some kids get *incredibly* stressed when they get thrown off of their ONE-TRACK THINKING.

Look at the two examples below and think about how you would react. Then write or check your answers.

Example 1

Peter loves to talk about World War II airplanes. He can tell you the name, flying height, speed, and special abilities of every type of plane used in the war. Peter is in history class and the class is discussing the Ancient Romans. Peter gets excited during the discussion and begins to interrupt. He starts talking about how the Roman wars were similar to World War II and then begins to talk again about the airplanes used in the war.

The teacher stops him and says, "Peter! Enough about World War II planes! We are talking about the Romans now. If you can't talk about the Romans and if you keep interrupting, I will have to send you to the principal!"

How does Peter feel when the teacher tells him to stop talking about airplanes?

_____

Do you think this causes Peter to feel stress?　□ YES　　□ NO

Has something like this ever happened to you?　□ YES　　□ NO

How do **you** feel when this sort of thing happens?

_____

Example 2

Alicia walks the same way to school every day. She turns down Maple Street, makes a right on Beech Street, takes Beech to the end, makes a left on to Oak – and her school is on the right hand side. One day, Alicia turns down Maple, makes a right on Beech, but when she goes to the end, she can't make a left unto Oak. It is blocked off by the police because a tree has fallen down. She now has to go back up Beech and take another street to get over to her school. She isn't expecting this, and it is almost time for the school bell to ring.

How does Alicia feel when she sees that the road is blocked?

_____

Do you think this causes Alicia to feel stress? ☐ YES ☐ NO

Has something like this ever happened to you? ☐ YES ☐ NO

How do **you** feel when this sort of thing happens?

_____

Now it's your turn. Think of a time when your ONE-TRACK Thinking didn't work. Maybe you had to stop talking about your favorite topic. Maybe you got lost. Maybe the teacher changed where you sit in class without warning you. Maybe you had a test in history and were expecting questions about facts (which you are very good at) but the teacher asked you about your opinion instead.

This is what happened to me: _____

_____

_____

_____

How much stress did this cause?

☐ None   ☐ A Little   ☐ Some   ☐ A lot   ☐ A whole lot

> *Don't worry if you think that you have a lot of trouble with One-Track Thinking. Everybody can think this way once in a while. In Chapter 5, you will learn how to think in a more flexible and less stressful way.*

Difficulty With Making FRIENDS

This isn't a book that is mostly about how to make friends or learning social skills. This is a book about managing stress. But problems with making friends can cause a lot of stress. Here are some of the problems that kids have with getting along with others:

🌀 Being bullied

🌀 Being teased

🌀 Unable to understand "the rules" of playing

🌀 Being left out

🌀 Not invited to fun events

🌀 No one to play with at recess

🌀 Feeling forced by parents/teachers/counselors to "make friends"

🌀 Not having other kids that you can share your problems with

QUESTION: What does all this have to do with stress?

ANSWER: Scientists have discovered what many people have known for a long time:

Having friends can help to reduce stress.

Friends can help when you are feeling sad, nervous, or upset. It also feels good when you know that there are other people who like you and want to be around you. Having friends can also help you to learn new things, to go to new places, and to try new activities. Besides, bullies tend to stay away from kids who have friends (they like to go after the kid who is all alone).

You may be much better at getting along with adults than you are with other kids. Adults can be easier to talk to and are willing to listen when you talk about your interests. It's great that you can get along with adults. Adults such as parents, grandparents, teachers, and counselors can be very helpful in many different ways. But there are some things that you can get from kids your own age that you just can't get from adults.

Let's look at YOUR friendships.

Chapter 1: What Makes Me Stressed?

Complete the circle on the next page as follows:

1. Put your name in the center circle.

2. In the next surrounding circle, put the names of your *Best Friends.* A best friend is someone that you spend a lot of time with, that you can trust, that you can talk to about important things, and that you have a lot in common with (you like a lot of the same things).

3. In the next surrounding circle, put the name of your *Friends.* These are kids that you know and spend some time with. You are usually invited to their birthday parties. However, they aren't considered "best friends."

4. In the next surrounding circle, put your *Acquaintances* (ah-quay-ten-says). These are kids you see often (for example, classmates, kids you might see in chorus or karate class, and so on). You may say "hi" to these kids and even talk a little with them, but you haven't been over to their house. You may like these kids, but they are not really your friends (at least not yet!).

My Friendships

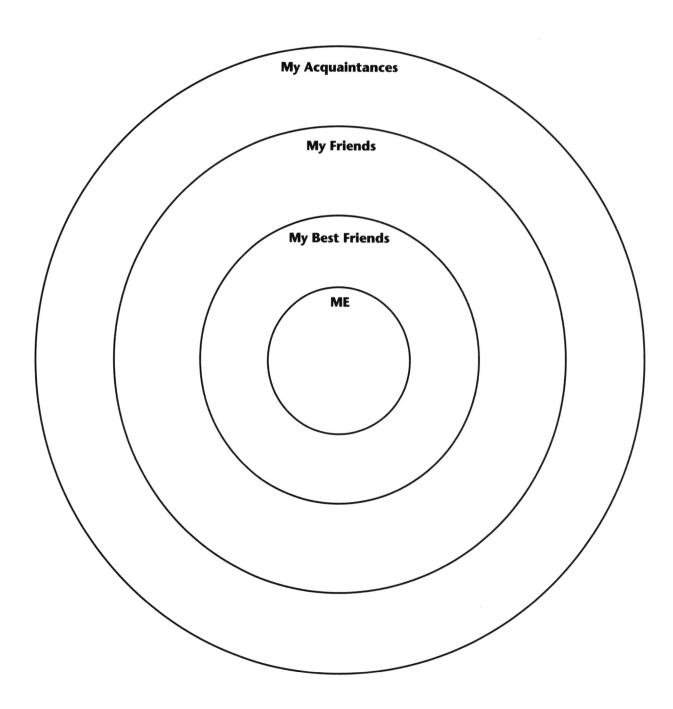

My Acquaintances

My Friends

My Best Friends

ME

Chapter 1: What Makes Me Stressed?

Look at your social circle and answer these questions:

How many people, in total, do you have in all circles? _____

Do you think you would feel better if you had more people in your circles?

☐ YES   ☐ NO

Explain: _____

_____

_____

Is there anyone in the Acquaintances circle that you would like to have in the Friends circle?

☐ YES   ☐ NO

Is there anyone in the Friends circle that you would like to have in the Best Friends circle.

☐ YES   ☐ NO

Has anyone moved towards the outer circles (for example, at one time they were a Best Friend but *now* you consider them to be an Acquaintance)?

☐ YES   ☐ NO

If YES, explain what happened. _____

_____

_____

Don't worry too much if you don't have many friends listed. It's not how many friends you have that's important. What's more important is how strong the friendships are that you do have. But it can be useful to have different kinds of friends and different levels of friendships. This can help you to be more connected with the world. In Chapter 9, you will learn ideas and skills to help you get along better with other kids. This will help to reduce your stress level.

Overloaded SENSES

Sensory sensitivities can also make kids feel stressed and nervous.

The senses are things like:
@ Sight

@ Smell

@ Taste

@ Touch

@ Hearing

@ Balance and movement

When you have a sensory sensitivity, it can be hard to control how much you feel with your senses. Sometimes you may feel too much. Sometimes you may not feel enough. For example:

 Some kids are very sensitive to light. You may find certain kinds of light bulbs to be annoying or even painful to your eyes.

 Some kids are very sensitive to all kinds of smells. You may find one smell in particular to be super disgusting (for example, the smell of a banana) or you may find many smells to be nasty.

 Some kids may only eat certain kinds of food. You may find that a lot of foods taste horrible – you may even get sick if you are forced to eat certain foods. You may end up eating only one type of food (for example, only bread and pasta) or even only one very specific food (for example, only chicken nuggets).

Chapter 1: What Makes Me Stressed?

 Some kids are very sensitive when it comes to their sense of touch. You may not like the feel of certain clothing. You may hate having tags on your shirts. You may jump a mile if touched by surprise. Some kids are <u>under</u>-sensitive to touch. That means they don't feel touch much or almost not at all. This can be dangerous if your brain does not know when you are hurt.

 Some kids are very sensitive to sounds. You may not like any loud sounds at all. For example, you may find it too noisy to be at a baseball game or at a school assembly. There may also be certain kinds of sounds that you can't stand (for example, the sound of a vacuum cleaner).

 Some kids have problems with the sensations of balance and movement. You may feel the need to swing or spin or you may have problems with bumping into things and falling.

QUESTION: Why are sensory problems discussed in this book?

ANSWER: Because sensory sensitivities can make life VERY stressful. Even something as simple as walking from class to class can be difficult for a kid with sensory sensitivities (think of the noises, the crowd, and the need for balance and movement). Some sensitivities can cause PANIC. Some kids are so sensitive to tastes and smells that they actually throw up just by seeing some foods or by smelling something unusual. They may also be getting pressure from parents and others to eat different foods or to "forget" about things that bother them like sounds and touch. All of this causes stress.

Take a moment to think about YOUR sensory profile. The things that make you uncomfortable, the things you can deal with, and the things that are completely disturbing.

My Sensory Profile

Sights I Like	Sights That Make Me Uncomfortable	Sights I CAN'T STAND!
Smells I Like	Smells That Make Me Uncomfortable	Smells I CAN'T STAND!
Tastes I Like	Tastes That Make Me Uncomfortable	Tastes I CAN'T STAND!
Feelings (Touch) I Like	Feelings (Touch) That Make Me Uncomfortable	Feelings (Touch) I CAN'T STAND!
Sounds I Like	Sounds That Make Me Uncomfortable	Sounds I CAN'T STAND!
Movements I Like (movements are things like bike riding, swinging on a swing, or riding on a roller coaster)	Movements That Make Me Uncomfortable	Movements I CAN'T STAND!

Take a look at your chart. I bet that the things that you CAN'T STAND have caused you a lot of stress at one time or another!

Problems Caused by My Sensory Sensitivities (fill in the blanks):

Sense	Problems Caused by Sensitivities
Sound	
Sight	
Taste	
Smell	
Touch	
Balance/Movement	

Being aware of the types of sensations that make you feel uncomfortable can help you start to deal with those kinds of problems. You can learn things to do when you are uncomfortable (you will learn this in Chapter 3 and Chapter 4). You will also learn a way to solve problems in Chapter 6 and you can use this to work on your sensory sensitivities.

Being aware of the types of sensations that make you feel uncomfortable can help you start to deal with those kinds of problems. You can learn things to do when you are uncomfortable (you will learn this in Chapter 3 and Chapter 4). You will also learn a way to solve problems in Chapter 6 and you can use this to work on your sensory sensitivities.

Problems at SCHOOL

Let's look at three areas of school that can be a problem:
1. The work
2. The school
3. The students

The Work

Most kids are really good at some things in school and need to work harder to learn other things. For example, one kid may be really good at math but not so good at spelling, and for another kid it may be just the opposite. Some of the kinds of problems that kids may have with learning include …

Problems With Fine-Motor Skills
Fine-motor skills have to do with movements that require a lot of planning and coordination. Think of things like using scissors, tying your shoes, and riding a bicycle. These things might have been hard for you to learn. As kids get older, this problem is usually seen at school in one area especially: handwriting. Writing may be hard for you; your hands may even hurt when you have to write for a long time.

Problems With Understanding Certain Sayings
"You're pushing my buttons," "It's raining cats and dogs," "That's walking a fine line" – kids sometimes have difficulty with understanding sayings like these. For some kids, words mean what they are supposed to mean and that's that. So it can get pretty confusing when words are used to mean something different than what you expect.

Problems With Understanding Social and Emotional Ideas
Sometimes rules about feelings and playing with others do not make a lot of sense. For example, think about these two rules:
Rule #1: *It's not O.K. to tell someone they look very old – even if it's true.*
Rule #2: *It's wrong to lie, and you should always tell the truth.*

How can you have *both* rules? This is the confusing part. It can be hard to know when a rule should or shouldn't be used.

Understanding the emotions of others can also be hard. It's not that you don't care about others, but sometimes you may not understand *why* people feel the way that they do. These types of challenges can become a problem at school when you have to understand social and emotional rules to complete an assignment. Some examples include comparing characters in a book, understanding or writing poetry, and writing assignments that ask for more than facts.

Chapter 1: What Makes Me Stressed?

Problems With Organization
Problems with organization can happen in many different ways, including:

@ Things like books and assignments get lost.

@ You forget to bring things to or from school.

@ Papers get mixed up.

@ It's difficult to manage your time.

@ You do not "show" your work.

@ You lose your place when reading or doing math problems.

@ You do not know what's important to study and what is less important.

@ You lose track of when assignments are due.

Problems With Paying Attention
Kids who have problems with paying attention are easily distracted. It may also be difficult to listen to someone talk for a long time. You may mix up directions or only get part of a direction. Some kids get very squirmy when they have to listen for a long time and may not be able to stay in their seat for very long.

Attention problems are usually worse when you have to do something that *someone else* wants you to do or when you have to listen to someone else. You may be great at sitting for hours while playing a video game, but this is something that YOU decided to do. In school, you don't always get to choose what you want to do.

Look back over the different types of problems described above. Which ones are problems for you (check the following)?

Problems With Fine-Motor Skills
☐ Not a problem   ☐ A little bit of a problem   ☐ A BIG problem

Problems With Understanding Certain Sayings
☐ Not a problem   ☐ A little bit of a problem   ☐ A BIG problem

Problems With Understanding Social and Emotional Ideas
☐ Not a problem   ☐ A little bit of a problem   ☐ A BIG problem

Problems With Organization
☐ Not a problem   ☐ A little bit of a problem   ☐ A BIG problem

Problems With Paying Attention
☐ Not a problem   ☐ A little bit of a problem   ☐ A BIG problem

The School

Schools can be noisy, crowded, and very confusing places. Take a look at the list below and check (√) the things about school that you find stressful:

_____	Bells ringing
_____	Not having enough time to get from class to class
_____	Teachers too loud
_____	Hallways too crowded
_____	The school smelling bad
_____	Can't find your way around
_____	Having to go outside for gym
_____	Having to eat in the noisy cafeteria
___√___	Uncomfortable desks
___√___	Class periods too long
_____	Too many distractions in class
_____	Assemblies
_____	Class trips

Now it's YOUR turn. You get to design your very own school on the next page!

Think about your idea of the perfect school.

@ Is your school large or small?

@ How many students are in your classes?

@ How is your school building different from most other school buildings? For example, maybe it is round instead of rectangular, maybe it has windows everywhere or no windows at all, maybe it has huge rooms or very small rooms, or maybe there is a wildlife park in the center of the school. Use your imagination!

@ Where is your school located? Is it close to home or far away from home? Is it near a park? Near a beach?

@ What color is your school (inside and out)? Maybe it is multicolored or just black and white?

@ How about the cafeteria? What do they serve? Do they need to have an outdoor barbecue grill? A taco stand? Maybe it's like a food court? And what about the seats? Big tables or small tables? Big chairs with their own entertainment system? Go ahead and dream!

@ What about the playground? What kinds of equipment does it have? How large or small is the playground?

Chapter 1: What Makes Me Stressed?

This is a diagram of my ideal school (draw and paste in pictures):

```



```

Take a look at your ideal school and think about how different it is from your real school. This will help you to understand some of the ways that the school building may be stressful for you. You may not be able to change your school in a big way, but think about how you may be able to make it at least a little bit better. Examples of things you may be able to change (*with parent and teacher permission*) include:

- Changing your seat to avoid distractions (for example, you don't want to look out of the window while the teacher is talking)
- Walking a different way to and from class to avoid noisy hallways
- Being the first or last person to leave the class to avoid bumping into others
- Staying away from "smelly" areas
- Staying in quieter areas in the cafeteria and on the playground

The Students

Most of the kids at your school are nice. However, nobody gets along with everybody all of the time. As for most students, there will be at least some kids who you find to be annoying.

- There may be noisy kids in your class who often don't listen to the teacher. These kids can be distracting, and it is hard to listen to the teacher yell at these kids all day.

- You may feel responsible for telling the teacher if someone breaks "the rules" at school. If so, having a bunch of kids around who don't follow the rules can be very stressful.

- There may be bullies in your school, and this can be a big problem. These are kids who tease you and may even try to hurt you. It can be pretty scary having to deal with bullies and definitely very stressful.

Now take a "true" or "false" quiz to see how stressful the other students are at your school.

TRUE or FALSE (circle the correct answer)

There are a lot of bullies at my school.	True	False
The kids at my school are very distracting to me.	True	False
The kids at school don't let me play with them.	True	False
There is too much pushing and shoving in the hallway.	True	False
The other kids break the rules all of the time.	True	False
Some of the kids make fun of me.	True	False
I don't know how to play with the other kids.	True	False

Answering "True" to any one of these statements may mean that the other kids are adding to your stress. Sometimes the other kids are doing things to bother you on purpose, but most of the time they may not know that what they are doing is bothering you.

Although school can be stressful, it is a very important part of your life. The ideas and skills that you will learn in this book will help you to deal with a lot of the things that make you stressed at school.

Having Different Talents and Interests

Wait a minute! How can having a talent be a bad thing? It's not! But it can become stressful if your talent and interests are very different from the other kids'. For example, many kids are really into sports, but you may not be. So, you may not get picked to be on teams, you may feel embarrassed when you play sports, and you may feel left out if all the other kids are joining sports teams and you are not.

Also, many kids with sensitivities are smart – REALLY SMART. This also is not a bad thing! But sometimes it can be difficult to talk to the other kids in school because they don't know the same things that you do. You may know absolutely everything there is to know about computers, or civil war battles, or the *Titanic*, or robotics, or trains, or the migration routes of butterflies, or whatever. Other kids may not know as much about these things. They may find the stuff that you talk about boring and you may find the stuff that they talk about to be boring. This can become stressful over time as it is nice to have someone to talk to, and having things in common can make it much easier to become friends.

Let's take a look at some of the things that kids are interested in:

Things MOST kids are interested in:

ℯ Video games

ℯ Cartoons

ℯ Using cell phones (especially for texting)

ℯ Sports

ℯ Using computers for "social networking" (sites to communicate with other kids)

ℯ Listening to popular music

ℯ Bike riding

ℯ Reading popular kids' books

ℯ Collecting things like comic books and cards

Things SOME kids are interested in:

ℯ Chess

ℯ Band

ℯ Listening to classical music

ℯ Using computers to look up information for school

- ℮ Reading long books
- ℮ Acting
- ℮ Arts and crafts
- ℮ Going to museums
- ℮ Collecting things like stamps and coins

Things that ONLY A FEW kids are interested in:

- ℮ High-speed photography
- ℮ Memorizing long lists
- ℮ Using the computer to look up *very specific* facts (for example, miles between different cities)
- ℮ Collecting things like train ticket stubs or bus route maps
- ℮ Reading manuals for electrical appliances

Now answer these questions (check the boxes and write in the blanks):

Are you interested in something that MOST kids are interested in? ☐ YES ☐ NO

If YES, list those things here: _____

_____

Are you interested in something that SOME kids are interested in? ☐ YES ☐ NO

If YES, list those things here: _____

_____

Are you interested in things that ONLY A FEW kids are interested in? ☐ YES ☐ NO

If YES, list those things here: _____

_____

What are YOU really interested in? _____

_____

Do you think MOST, SOME, or ONLY A FEW kids are interested in the thing (or things) that you are really interested in? _____

If ONLY A FEW kids are interested in the same things that you are, does that cause you stress?

If YES, how? _____

_____

Although it may sometimes be stressful, having different talents can make life fun and interesting. In Chapter 10, you will learn how to use your talents (and other strengths) to help fight stress.

This chapter helped to show that there are a lot of situations that are more stressful for kids who have sensitivities. But you are not the only kid in the world who feels stress! EVERYBODY feels stressed at times. So everybody would benefit from learning different ways to deal with stress. This is what most of this book is about. But first we are going to talk about what exactly stress is – from a scientific point of view.

Congratulations!

You have earned your first two ice blocks.

You are on your way to building your Stress Management Igloo.

CHAPTER 2
THE SCIENCE OF STRESS

What is stress exactly? Good question! "Stress" is a word that we hear over and over again.

The word "stress" means different things to different people. Most people think of stress as something COMPLETELY HORRIBLE; something that we need to stay away from all the time. But not everybody thinks this way, and some people actually say they like stress (imagine that)!

Before we go any further, write down YOUR definition of stress. Don't worry about what other people have told you about stress – think about what the word means to YOU.

My definition of STRESS:

Stress is_____

_____

_____

Although there are many different ways of defining stress, there are six things for sure about stress.

1. Stress is something that has a REAL effect on minds and bodies.
2. Stress can happen from any CHANGE – whether good or bad.
3. Stress can happen from both real and IMAGINED events.
4. Some stress is GOOD.
5. Too much stress can be BAD.
6. You can learn to MANAGE your stress.

Let's look at each of these.

Stress Is Something That Has a REAL Effect on Minds and Bodies

Our nervous system helps us to think, feel, sense, and behave. Our nervous system is made up of our brain, spinal cord, and nerves.

Here is an interesting fact: Our nervous system runs in two different modes.

The first mode runs through what is known as the *sympathetic nervous system.*

When operating in this mode, our nervous system is ON ALERT. It senses that something is wrong and gets us ready for action. You can think of this as being our nervous system's HOT mode.

The second mode runs through what is known as the *parasympathetic nervous system.*

When operating in this mode, our nervous system is calm and relaxed. This mode helps us to get back to normal after we've been stressed in some way. You can think of this as being our nervous system's COOL mode.

The HOT Mode

Let's talk about the HOT mode first. Our nervous system's HOT mode can be very useful. If it wasn't for this part of our nervous system, we wouldn't become alarmed and ready when something dangerous was about to happen.

Now, answer this statement (circle):

You should never be scared; it just isn't useful: True   False

To help you answer this statement, think about this: Think about it ...

You are walking in the mountains when suddenly a huge grizzly bear comes charging out of the forest and is heading straight toward you.

What would YOU do? _____

_____

Without the HOT mode, you would continue to do what you were doing. You might even approach the bear and try to play with him!

That is not a good idea. In fact, you might end up as the bear's lunch.

Now, how does our nervous system's HOT mode help us in this situation? Our HOT mode gets our bodies ready for *fight or flight.* This means that in order to survive when we see something that is dangerous, we have to do one of two things:

1. We can fight the thing that is dangerous.
                    OR
2. We can run as fast was possible.

Our HOT mode doesn't decide for us whether we do 1 or 2, but it gets our bodies ready to do either one.

When to Run and When to Face Your Fear

What do you think would be the best response for these situations – fight or flight?

Circle One

@ You are crossing the road and see a truck speeding   Fight   Flight
toward you.

@ You are sitting in social studies class and the teacher   Fight   Flight
announces a pop quiz.

@ You are flying a kite and you see a bolt of lightning.   Fight   Flight

@ You are sitting alone at a lunch table and another kid   Fight   Flight
asks if he can join you.

> **Remember:** *Fight doesn't always mean that you are going to hit someone. It means that you are going to get ready to face something that might be challenging or scary.*

Sometimes choosing whether to fight or run is easy. You probably didn't decide to face that truck, run out of your social studies class, or stay outside in the thunderstorm. But the last situation is not quite as simple to figure out. Let's look at it a little more carefully.

At first, it would seem like a good idea to fight any feelings of shyness that you may have and invite the other kid to join you. But what if that other kid is known to be a bully? What if that other kid is a stranger? Sometimes the fight or flight decision isn't easy.

How does our nervous system's HOT mode get our bodies ready for fight or flight?

Quite a lot of stuff happens. All kinds of chemical reactions take place. These happen through stuff in our body like hormones and neurotransmitters (nur-ro-trans-mit-ers).

DON'T WORRY! You don't have to be an expert in chemistry to learn how to handle stress. What *is* important to know is that the HOT mode gets your body energized and ready for action.

Here are some of the things that happen:

℮ Your **heart** starts to beat faster.

℮ You start to **breathe** faster (this can make you feel dizzy or lightheaded).

℮ Your **muscles** tense up.

℮ You get extra **energy** (from chemicals in your bodies that come from tiny structures in your bodies called glands).

℮ You become more **alert**.

℮ You can **see** better, especially from the side (that's called peripheral vision).

℮ Your **stomach** stops working to break down your food (your energy is needed in other parts of your body), and you may start to feel a little sick ("butterflies in the stomach").

℮ You may start to **sweat**.

℮ Your **emotions** become stronger; you may become fearful and start to panic OR you may become very angry.

Although most of these things may seem "BAD," they can help when you are faced with a threat.

Fight or Flight in Action
Pretend that you are back in the old times, say the Middle Ages in Europe. You are a knight about to do battle. Your side is marching across the field and the enemy is marching toward you. As the two sides get closer and closer to doing battle, your nervous system's HOT mode starts to kick in.

Think about how your HOT mode may stop you from getting your head chopped off. In this battle (write in your answers below) …

1. Why would it be good to have extra energy?

    _____

    _____

2. Why would it be good to be more alert?

3. Why would it be good to see better from the side?

4. Is there anything else that your nervous system's HOT mode does that can help keep you alive? Pick another of the things that change in your body from the list above and explain how that will help you in battle:

The COOL Mode

The HOT mode does quite a lot. Now, let's find out what our nervous system's COOL mode does. Remember: The parasympathetic nervous system (our COOL mode) helps to keep the mind and body calm.

First, there is one really important fact about our nervous system's HOT and COOL modes:

**We cannot run in both
the HOT and COOL modes
at the same time!**

That means that when our HOT mode is running, our COOL mode is not, and when our COOL mode is running, our HOT mode is not.

Remember: Our nervous system's HOT mode gets us ready for action and our COOL mode helps us to relax. You can only be one **or** the other at any given time.

Circle One

Can you be angry and calm at the same time?   Yes   No

Can you be terrified and relaxed at the same time?   Yes   No

Our nervous system's HOT and COOL modes have two totally different jobs to do. This fact is going to be very important to remember when you learn about relaxation skills later in this book.

How Does the Parasympathetic Nervous System Help Our Bodies to Relax?

Many of things that the nervous system's COOL mode does to make you relaxed are just the opposite of what your HOT mode does. Here are some of the things that happen:

- Your **heart** begins to beat at a slower, more regular rate.
- You start to **breathe** slower and deeper.
- Your **muscles** loosen up.
- You become **less alert**.
- Your **stomach** gets back to digesting food.
- You **stop sweating.**
- Your body begins to **rest and recover** (from the damage that the HOT mode has done).
- Your **emotions** cool down. You feel relaxed and calm.

Now that you understand how your body reacts to stress, let's talk about some of the things that can make you stressed.

Stress Can Happen From Any CHANGE: Whether Good or Bad

It's not just bad things that can cause stress; good things can, too. Even stuff that you are looking forward to can cause your nervous system's HOT mode to take over. That's because you need energy and focus to get through both the good and the bad things that happen in your life.

Many kids get very upset when things change. Even a little change, like having a substitute teacher or getting Chinese food on Friday night instead of pizza, can make it seem as if your entire world has been turned upside down.

Sometimes the changes that make some kids really upset don't bother other kids as much. However, there are a lot of changes that EVERYBODY gets stressed out by. There are different kinds of changes. Changes can be: Big Changes, Little Changes, or Medium Changes.

Take a look at the list below and circle the changes that have happened to you over the past year.

BIG CHANGES

Someone Very Close to You Dies	Parents Get a Divorce	Moving House
You Have a Very Bad School Year	Mom or Dad Loses Job	Getting a Big Award
You Get a New Brother or Sister	Changing Schools	Caught in a Natural Disaster

MEDIUM CHANGES

Getting a New Dog or Cat	New Teacher	A Distant Relative Dies
Going on a Long Vacation	Joining a New Activity	

SMALL CHANGES

You Have a Birthday Party	A New Kid Joins Your Class
You Have to do a Book Report	You Get Your First Cell Phone
You Have a Band Recital	You Miss Two Days of School Because You Are Sick
You Get a New Scout Badge	You Have to Test for Your Yellow Belt in Karate
Report Cards Come Out	Summer Vacation is Starting

Did any of the **BIG, MEDIUM**, or SMALL changes listed above happen to you?

How many from the **BIG** Changes box? _____

How many from the **MEDIUM** Changes box? _____

How many from the SMALL Changes box? _____

Try to think of other changes that happened to you over the past year? Can you list at least one from each category?

Over the past year, a really **BIG** change that happened to me was:

_____

_____

Over the past year, a **MEDIUM** change that happened to me was:

_____

_____

Over the past year, a **SMALL** change that happened to me was:

_____

_____

What Does All This Stuff About Change Mean?

If you have a lot of changes in your life, you usually have a lot of stress. And as we have just seen, this could happen with both good and bad changes.

Sometimes you may see small changes as being BIG changes, so this can make your stress even worse. All it takes is one BIG change to feel a lot of stress. Three or four MEDIUM changes are usually enough to cause stress, and a whole bunch of SMALL changes happening around the same time can also do it.

Take a look at the things you checked above. Don't worry if you checked a lot. Most kids are experiencing a lot of change at this point in life. You may not be able to stop the number of changes that are happening in your life right now, but you *can* learn to manage your stress.

Stress Can Happen From Both Real and IMAGINED Events

In the last section, we talked about some real events that can cause stress. But did you know that you can also get stressed *just by what you are thinking about?* This is because our nervous system's HOT mode (our sympathetic nervous system) doesn't know the difference between what is real and what is in our imagination and neither does our nervous system's COOL mode (our parasympathetic nervous system), but more about that later.

So you can get stressed if you fail a test OR if you THINK about failing a test.

You can get stressed if your dog gets hurt OR if you WORRY about your dog getting hurt.

You can get stressed if you are in an accident OR if you IMAGINE yourself getting into an accident.

You can get stressed if you are caught in a tornado OR if you watch a television show about kids who get caught in a tornado.

You can get stressed if you are facing a two-headed, man-eating zombie from outer space OR if you if you have a nightmare about a two-headed, man-eating, zombie from outer space.

Now it's YOUR turn to give a couple of examples by writing them in the blanks below:

You can get stressed if you get sick OR _____

_____

You can get stressed if you strike out at baseball OR _____

_____

So you can get stressed by real things that happen to you or by things that you think about, worry over, imagine, watch on TV, or dream about.

Why is this important to know?

Because if you want to learn to manage stress, you must pay attention to two things:

1. The problems that you really have.
                    AND
2. The problems that you worry about having.

Here's another important idea:

You need to have some stress to accomplish really big things in life!

- You can't get great grades without studying hard.

- You can't be good at something without practicing a lot.

- Your team can't win the championship without playing some teams that are tough to beat.

- You can't make new friends without taking some chances.

Now think about one of your biggest accomplishments so far in life and write it down.

My accomplishment: _____

_____

_____

What did you have to do to reach this accomplishment? _____

_____

_____

Was it stressful at times to reach your accomplishment? ☐ YES ☐ NO

Was it worth it to reach your accomplishment? ☐ YES ☐ NO

Most of the time, even things that are hard to achieve are worth the effort.

So, some stress can be good and even make your life better and more exciting. You may ask, "Why am I even completing this workbook on stress management, if stress can be good?" Good question! That leads us to the next point about stress.

Too Much Stress Can Be BAD

We know that when we are under stress, our nervous system (through the HOT mode) does various things to get our bodies alert and ready for action. It's O.K. if this happens once in a while. In fact, scientists have discovered that it may be good for our bodies to get *a little* stressed now and then. But BAD things can happen to our bodies and our minds if we have too much stress.

Here are some of the things that too much stress can do to you. Check off the ones that happen to you:

☐ Feeling tense all the time   ☐ Can't get to sleep at night   ☐ Worry too much

☐ Can't pay attention in school   ☐ Headaches   ☐ Stomachaches

☐ Get sick a lot   ☐ Feel super nervous   ☐ Tired most of the time

☐ Go to the bathroom a lot   ☐ Very moody   ☐ Feel shaky

☐ Get angry all the time   ☐ Can't relax   ☐ Feeling kind of dizzy

☐ Hungry all the time   ☐ Don't feel like eating

How many did you check off? _____

Any one of these can be a warning sign that you are under too much stress. Some people show more than one of these warning signs. If you checked ANY of the warning signs, let your mom or dad know. Don't be embarrassed or afraid that your parents will get mad. Your parents *want* to know and they *want* to help.

How Much Stress Is TOO MUCH?

This is a tough question to answer. It depends on a lot of things, including …

@ How many stressful events are happening at the same time?

@ How many changes have you had to deal with recently?

@ How big were the changes?

@ What's your personality like? Are you usually a nervous person or are you usually more laid back?

@ What kind of help do you get from others (including family, friends, and teachers)?

@ Do you have any of the warning signs listed above?

@ Do you often feel that you just can't finish all the things you need to do?

Think about all of those questions and then answer this question:

I FEEL THAT I HAVE (circle one):

Very Little Stress in My Life   *Some* Stress in My Life   *Way TOO MUCH* Stress in My Life

Don't feel bad or different if you think that you have Way Too Much Stress in your life. There's a lot going on in your life right now, and it isn't always easy. Having sensitivities also can make life a lot more stressful (as we learned earlier). Many kids – *with or without* sensitivities – also feel very stressed (many adults feel the same way).

If you feel that you have Very Little or Some Stress in your life right now, that's great! But there are still some things you can learn by completing the rest of this book. EVERYBODY has to deal with stress sometimes. If you think that you have Way TOO MUCH stress, don't feel bad. Many kids feel this way. The things that you are going to learn from completing this workbook will be a big help.

And that leads to the most important point about stress …

You Can Learn to MANAGE Your Stress

What do you want to get out of completing this workbook? Check the following:

1. ☐ I want to get rid of ALL of my stress FOREVER.

2. ☐ I want to learn how to be TOTALLY relaxed and calm ALL OF THE TIME.

3. ☐ I want to be the WORLD'S BEST at EVERYTHING!!!!

4. ☐ I don't want to have any kind of sensitivities ever again.

5. ☐ I want to learn how to be more relaxed.

6. ☐ I want to learn some tips and strategies to help me manage my time better.

7. ☐ I want to learn how to live a life that includes both challenging activities and time to just chill out.

8. ☐ I don't know; my mom is making me read this book!

Completing this book cannot help you with any of the first three reasons. This is a book about how to manage your stress. It cannot help you to cure or get rid of stress forever. Nobody can do that because stress is part of your life (and everyone else's life, too!).

Managing your stress does NOT mean that you will be completely relaxed all the time or that you will become so laid back and chilled that you don't do anything challenging or difficult ever again. It means that you learn to live a more balanced life with time and energy for both relaxation and hard work. It also means that when you do start to feel stressed, you will have a number of skills or tips that you can use to feel more balanced again.

Completing this book also can't help you if you picked number 4. Having sensitivities is part of who you are, but it is not the whole part. Above all, you are a person – with your own thoughts, feelings, and dreams. But having sensitivities can make life more difficult at times. However, you can learn to live with your sensitivities and you can learn to feel good about the many strengths and talents that you have.

If you picked number 5, 6, or 7, completing this book can definitely help you.

If you picked the last one, hang on and give it a try … you may be pleasantly surprised by what you learn!

Congratulations!

You have earned two more ice blocks.

CHAPTER 3
RELAXATION
PART 1: RELAXING
MY BODY

Do you remember the difference between our nervous system's HOT and COOL modes? Here is a quick review.

Our nervous system's HOT mode gets our body ready for action. Sometimes this can be very helpful (and even save our lives – remember the case of the grizzly bear?). But sometimes, running in the HOT mode for too long causes us to be stressed and nervous.

Our nervous system's COOL mode helps our bodies to calm down after we have been stressed. Whatever the HOT mode has done to our bodies to get us ready for action, our COOL mode does the opposite so that we can relax again.

Remember the relationship between the HOT and COOL modes? We cannot run in both the HOT and the COOL modes at the same time! That's good news for dealing with stress. We can actually trick our bodies into turning on our COOL mode. If we can turn on our COOL mode, then the HOT mode turns off and we are much calmer.

QUESTION: How do we trick our bodies into turning on our nervous system's COOL mode?

ANSWER: By doing just the opposite of what our HOT mode does to our bodies.

Some things that our HOT mode does to our bodies, we can't control. For example, you can't usually control your heartbeat, vision, or the way that your stomach is working. However, you *can* control your breathing and you *can* control how tense your muscles are. And by doing so, you can control your stress!

Let's start by taking a look at breathing, but first we need to talk about the importance of practice.

The Importance of Practice

Relaxation is a skill, and just like any other skill, it must be learned and practiced. Although it may seem strange, you will have to put some work into being able to relax. The good news is that it's not difficult to learn some really good relaxation skills. Just remember the importance of practice. Think of all the things in life that you have gotten better at – chess, music, computers, whatever. Now think of all the hours of practice you put into getting better at these things. You didn't become good overnight. It's the same with relaxation. The more you practice, the better you will get.

Two relaxation techniques that are easy to learn and that work pretty well are *deep breathing* and *progressive muscle relaxation*. Let's spend some time learning about these techniques. Let's start with deep breathing.

Deep Breathing

Sit up in a comfortable chair and place your hand on your stomach (right over your belly button is fine). Now, take in a DEEP BREATH.

Did your hand move at all? If so, did it move in or out? If your hand moved outward, this means that you are breathing by filling up your entire lungs from the belly up. Congratulations! You are taking a full, deep breath. If your hand didn't move very much or if your hand moved inward, don't worry! You are breathing like nearly everyone else.

The problem with this kind of breathing is that you are only filling up part of your lungs with air. You are breathing from the upper chest area and not fully using your lungs.

We don't only need oxygen to survive; we also need it to relax. When we don't breathe the right way, we don't get enough oxygen, and when we don't get enough oxygen, all kinds of weird and bad things can happen. We can begin to feel panicky, dizzy, and light-headed. This makes us even more nervous, and then our breathing gets even worse.

It looks something like this:

Stress → Poor Breathing → Panicky Feelings → More Stress → Breathing Gets Even Worse → Panicky Feelings Worsen → And So On …………

This pattern can happen very quickly. Within seconds, you can begin to become very stressed and even panic.

So how do we stop this from happening?

Luckily, if we can control our breathing, we can control our stress levels. Remember what we know about our nervous system's HOT and COOL modes. Breathe poorly and our HOT mode turns on to make us nervous. Breathe deeply and slowly and the COOL mode turns on to calm us down.

Poor breathing usually means two things:

1. **Shallow breathing:** This means we breathe from the upper chest area and don't fill up our lungs completely.

2. **Rapid breathing:** This means we breathe in short, quick gasps.

If that is poor breathing, what is good breathing? Just take the opposite of the above.

The opposite of shallow is _____.

The opposite of rapid is _____.

So, the key is to learn to take slow, deep breaths. Taking slow breaths is easy – just slow down. But how do we take deep breaths? That's where diaphragmatic (di-a-fra-ma-tick) breathing comes in.

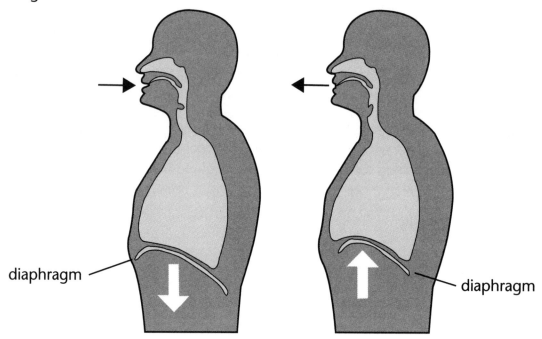

diaphragm

diaphragm

The diaphragm is a muscle found near the bottom of the lungs. If you lower and stretch this muscle, you can get more oxygen to your lungs. When you do this, your stomach usually pushes outward as you breathe in and then it usually pulls back in as you breathe out.

Try this exercise, but talk to an adult first!

1. Get a small book (not too heavy but not too light).
2. Lie on a comfortable floor (one with carpet would be best/if not use a pillow for your head).
3. Place the book over your belly button.
4. Close your eyes and take in a slow breath (you can breathe in with your mouth, your nose, or both if you like).
5. As you breathe in, allow your lungs to "drop" and expand so that the book rises slowly.
6. Wait 1 second when you have breathed in fully.

7. Breathe out slowly through your mouth.

    a. As you breathe out, blow the air out slowly through your lips; pretend you are blowing on a spoon of hot soup – if you blow too fast the soup will spill all over the place.

    b. As your breathe out, the book should slowly fall. Gently suck your stomach in as you push all of the air out.

8. Repeat breathing like this for at least five times.

Caution!
After you have done this exercise, make sure that you stand up slowly. Feeling a little light-headed or dizzy when you first start doing this exercise is normal. If you feel very uncomfortable, stop and breathe normally again and talk to an adult about it. Most people find breathing like this very relaxing. However, it is not for everyone. Don't worry if it makes you uncomfortable; there are plenty of other relaxation strategies that you can try.

Answer the following questions (by checking) to help decide if this type of breathing would be of any use to you in relaxing:

Were you able to do the breathing exercise? ☐ YES ☐ NO

If your answer is NO, what problems did you have?

☐ I couldn't breathe slowly.

☐ I couldn't expand my lungs properly.

☐ I couldn't blow out through my lips.

☐ I felt like I couldn't get enough air.

☐ Other problems? Explain: _____

In your own words, how did the exercise make you feel?_____

_____

Do you think this exercise will be helpful to you? ☐ YES ☐ NO

If you answered NO, don't worry! Most people find this type of breathing relaxing, but not everybody. If it doesn't work for you, try something else to relax. Just remember, all of these skills take practice. They may work only a little at the beginning, but *after practicing* you become better at them and they begin to work better and better.

Plan for Practice

It is usually best if you spend at least 10 minutes per day practicing this type of breathing. Practice when you can find a quiet time and place. It's not always easy finding a quiet time and place, but many people find the early night time to be the best. Just don't do it right before bedtime because you may be too tired to concentrate on the skill (and you just may fall asleep!).

Let's come up with a plan for how you can practice your breathing:

Time of day I should be able to practice: _____

Quiet place where I should be able to practice: _____

Amount of time I should be able to practice per day: _____

Tell an adult that you are planning to do this!

Using Deep Breathing in Real-Life Situations

Learning deep breathing can be useful, but you also have to learn how to use deep breathing when you need it the most: When you are stressed.

You may not always have a quiet place where you can lie down on the floor, place a book on your stomach, and begin to breathe like a Kung-Fu master. However, after you have practiced deep breathing for a while, you can do it without anyone noticing.

Practice deep breathing while sitting or standing. Instead of using a book for feedback, use your hand. Place a hand over your belly button and make sure that your hand moves outward as you breathe in and back inward as you breathe out. Next, try to breathe this way without using your hand. You will find that you are still able to take a nice, slow, deep breath without anyone being able to notice.

So, whenever you're in any sort of stressful situation, just try to take slow, deep breaths. Even though you may not be able to breathe as slowly or as deeply as you do while practicing in that quiet room or place, you can still do it enough so that it helps.

Muscle Relaxation

Your nervous system's HOT mode makes your muscles VERY TIGHT. This is known as "muscle tension." Sometimes you can actually feel how tight your muscles are, but usually you aren't even aware of your muscles being tight. However, if you're stressed, they probably are.

> **Remember:** *We can turn on our nervous system's COOL mode if we do the opposite of what the HOT mode does. So if our HOT mode makes our muscles TIGHT, we can get our COOL mode to turn on by making our muscles LOOSE.*

It may help you to understand the difference between TENSE and LOOSE muscles by thinking about the difference between a robot and a rag-doll.

   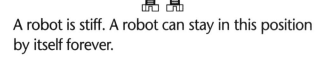

A rag doll is loose. It is floppy and needs someone to hold it up.

A robot is stiff. A robot can stay in this position by itself forever.

You may also think of your muscles as being like rubber bands.

When you stretch a rubber band, you can feel how tight it becomes. It feels like it is going to snap. When you let the rubber band go, it becomes loose and floppy. There is no longer any tension left in the rubber band.

So, how do we learn to make our muscles loose during times of stress?

Luckily, there is a great technique for this known as *progressive muscle relaxation*. Don't worry. It's not as complicated as it sounds.

Basically, progressive muscle relaxation (PMR for short) means that you focus on different muscles, making them tense, and then making them loose and relaxed. By doing this, you learn how to notice when your muscles are tensing up. You also get better at making them relaxed. If you practice enough, your muscles will be looser all the time and you will be feeling more relaxed.

> **Caution**
> *Do these exercises SLOWLY. If you feel any pain, stop this exercise IMMEDIATELY and let your parents know. If you have any kind of health problem, check with your parents first before trying these.*

Parents: *Check with your child's pediatrician and/or specialists if there are any relevant health concerns.*

The PMR Exercise

Find a quiet place and sit in a comfortable chair. Start by taking five slow, deep breaths. Then go through the muscle groups discussed below. At each group, make your muscles tense by pulling them together very tightly. Try to make them feel like a rubber band that is about to snap. Hold them at the tense position for 5 seconds. Then make your muscles go loose. Feel how relaxed they are when you let go. Keep them loose for at least 10 seconds; then go on to the next exercise. Do each muscle group twice.

Here are some of the movements you can do:

- Pretend that you have picked up a ball in your right hand. Squeeze it as tightly as you can; hold it for 5 seconds, then let go and relax the muscles for at least 10 seconds. Do the same with your left hand. Do both hands two times.

- Stretch your arms straight ahead. Stretch them as far as they can go. Feel the tension. Hold this for 5 seconds, then let go. Let your arms hang naturally and notice how loose they now feel. Do this twice.

- Close your eyes tightly. Feel all the muscles around your eyes and your forehead become very tense. Hold this for 5 seconds, then let go. Let your muscles smoothe out and feel relaxed.

- Press your lips together very tightly. You will feel tension in your lips and in your jaw. Hold this for 5 seconds, then let go. Let your mouth open slightly and feel how loose your lips and jaw have become. Repeat this.

- Slowly raise your shoulders. Keep your head straight and try to touch your ears with your shoulders (you won't really be able to touch your ears!). Feel all the tension in your neck muscles. Hold for 5 seconds and then relax. Let your shoulders drop and try to let your neck muscles relax. Repeat this movement.

- Arch your back by making it curve. Pull your arms in and push your elbows back. Feel the tension. Hold for 5 seconds and then relax. Repeat.

- Stick your legs straight out. Feel the tension throughout your legs and into your feet. Hold for 5 seconds and then let go. Let your legs drop and think about making them as loose as possible. Repeat.

- Finish by taking five more deep breaths. Think about what your body now feels like. If you feel any part of your body is tense, try your best to relax that body part. Try to think of words that will help you like "calm," "relax," "loose," or "smooth."

Other Movements

There are many other kinds of movements that you can do. If you are interested, you and your parents can look at some of the following websites:

A site from the Your Family Clinic/Holistic Psychology Website:
http://www.yourfamilyclinic.com/adhd/relax.htm

A site from the Children's Anxiety Institute:
http://childrenwithanxiety.com/articles-resources/how-to-teach-children-progressive-muscle-relaxation

A site from Kids' Relaxation.com Website:
http://kidsrelaxation.com/category/progressive-relaxation/

No matter what movements you decide to do, remember: Really notice what it feels like to be tense and then really think about what it feels like to be loose. And remember: **Never do any movement that hurts.**

Now let's think about how useful this exercise may be for *you*.

Were you able to do the exercise?　　☐ YES　　☐ NO

If your answer is NO, what problems did you have (use √)?

☐ I couldn't make my muscles tense.

☐ I couldn't make my muscles loose.

☐ It hurt.

☐ I couldn't concentrate long enough.

☐ Other problems? Explain: _____

In your own words, how did the exercise make you feel? _____

_____

Do you think this exercise will be helpful to you?　　☐ YES　　☐ NO

If you think this would be useful, make a plan to practice.

> ***TIP:*** *You can practice your PMR at the same time that you practice your deep breathing.*

My Plan for Practice

Time of day I should be able to practice: _____

Quiet place where I should be able to practice: _____

Amount of time I should be able to practice per day: _____

Tell an adult about your plan.

Other Ways to Relax the Body

All through history, people have invented ways of calming their minds by calming their bodies. They have known that it is hard to be stressed when your body is telling you that all is well.

Let's look at two skills that have been used for centuries: Yoga and tai chi. Both of these skills are best learned in a class with a trained teacher.

Yoga

Yoga began hundreds of years ago in India. When you do yoga exercises, you slowly stretch your body into different shapes. These shapes are called yoga poses. It is very important that you breathe the right way as you do these exercises (like we talked about before: slowly and deeply). If you really like yoga, you may want to try a class (check with your parents). There are many places where you can find a good yoga teacher. Remember: Just like the progressive muscle relaxation, DO NOT do anything that hurts. Do these exercises SLOWLY. And when you start out, do it with an adult.

Mountain

Stand with your feet together. Keep your hands down by your sides and look forward. Stretch your fingers down towards the floor. Take in a deep breath. As you breathe in, raise your arms straight over your head and hold them there for a few breaths. Once you feel loose, you can continue to stretch and hold your arms up and down. Breathe in as you lift your arms over your head and breathe out as you lower them again.

Cat and Dog

Get down on your hands and knees. Keep your hands just in front of your shoulders. As you breathe in, tilt your pelvis and tailbone (the butt bones!) upward and let your spine curve downward. Drop the stomach low and lift your head up. This is the dog position. As you breathe out, move your spine up and pull your chest and stomach in. You should now look like a cat that is mad or afraid (with the hairs on its back standing up). This is the cat position. Move slowly and smoothly from cat to dog and then back into cat. Repeat this movement several times. Don't forget the breathing.

Cobra

Lie down on your stomach. Keep your legs together and your arms at your side with your hands by your chest. Breathe in and slowly raise your chest and head as high as they will go. Keep your head up and chest out. Breathe out and slowly go back down. Repeat this movement; breathe in as you go up and out as you go back down.

Tree

Stand tall with your feet together. Raise your right foot and bend the knee while keeping your other leg firmly on the ground. Try to place the bottom of your right foot on the inside of the left leg. Go as high as you are comfortable and make sure that you don't go so high that you lose your balance and fall. Imagine that roots are growing from your left leg down into the ground. Press your hands together like you are praying. If you feel very balanced, you can reach your arms over your head and pretend that your arms and fingers are growing branches. Repeat this for the other side.

Tai Chi

Tai chi is like yoga in a lot of ways. In both yoga and tai chi, you stretch and you focus on your breathing. However, in tai chi, you move slowly rather than standing still. Also, in tai chi, you think about moving your life energy (what is called "chi") throughout your body. This is an important part of tai chi. If you are interested in learning tai chi, there may be a class with a trained teacher nearby (check with your parents). Here is one exercise for you to try. The first time, do it with an adult.

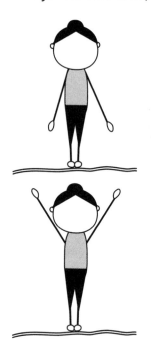

Flying Wild Goose

Stand with your knees slightly bent, arms at your side. Take in a deep breath and raise your arms by leading with your elbows (like you are flying) and standing up straight like you are ready to take off. Breathe out. As you breathe out, slowly lower your arms and get back down to how you started. Do this slowly and picture your energy moving up and back through your body.

Other Things You Can Do to Relax

There are many other things you can do to relax your body. Some of them may be things that you do every day. However, if you are very stressed, you should practice at least one of the skills above. Remember: **Practice, Practice, Practice**.

Check off some of the things you like to do to relax:

☐ Take a bath   ☐ Go for a walk   ☐ Play with your pets

☐ Play a sport   ☐ Play a board game   ☐ Take a nap

☐ Talk with someone   ☐ Listen to music   ☐ Read

☐ Other: _____

Now that you know how to relax your body, in the next chapter, let's see how you can relax your mind.

Congratulations!

You have earned two more ice blocks.

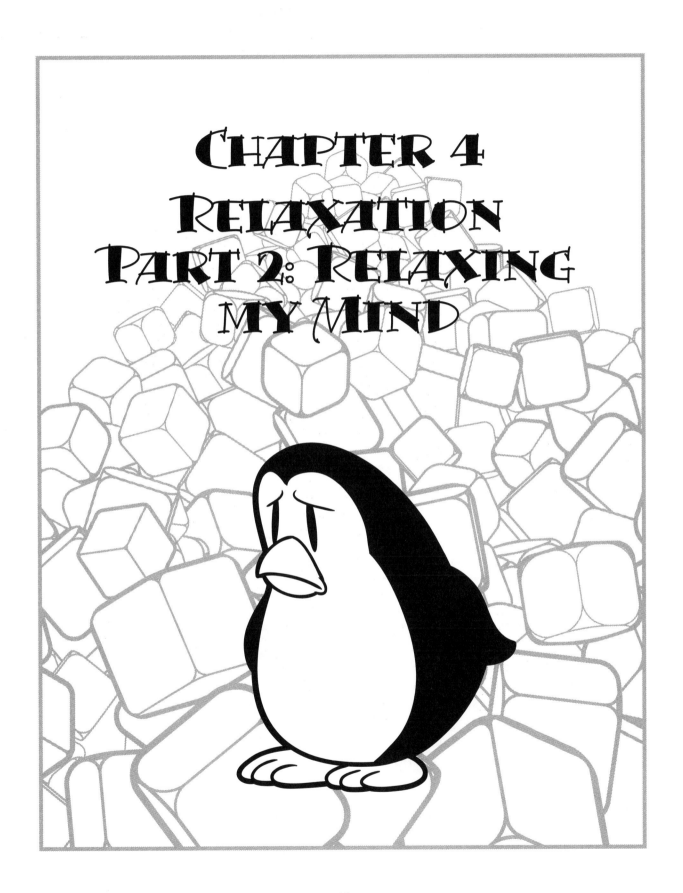

CHAPTER 4
RELAXATION
PART 2: RELAXING
MY MIND

When you are stressed, your mind does all sorts of things. You may start to worry about the same thing over and over again. You may picture something in your head that you fear will happen in the future. You may have all kinds of bummer thoughts such as "I can't deal with this." When people get very nervous about something, they can quickly begin to think the worst:

@ If you can't find your cereal in the morning, you may think, "This is the WORST day ever!"

@ Right before a test, you may think, "I just know I'm going to fail."

@ Before you go to the school dance, you may think, "This is going to be horrible!"

When you are stressed, your nervous system's HOT mode (or sympathetic nervous system) kicks in.

When your nervous system's HOT mode takes over, you begin to worry, imagine scary things, and think that the worst is about to happen. Remember your nervous system's HOT mode thinks that something really dangerous is about to happen and this is your body's way of trying to warn you. The problem is that the dangerous thing isn't real – it's your mind playing tricks on you.

To calm your HOT mode down, you need to call on your nervous system's COOL mode (or parasympathetic nervous system).

Remember: *Your nervous system cannot run in both modes at the same time.*

Your nervous system's COOL mode helps you to think calming thoughts. It's as if your COOL mode is saying relaxing things to you and helping you to imagine calming scenes. So, if you can think calming thoughts, say relaxing things to yourself, or imagine something that is calming to you, then you help to switch your nervous system from the HOT mode to the COOL mode.

What are some ways that you can think relaxing thoughts? In this chapter we are going to discuss two ways to relax the mind:

• Imagery

• Meditation

Imagery

Can you picture the following in your mind?

🌀 A big, flowing river

🌀 A dog barking

🌀 The smell of popcorn

🌀 The feel of wind on your face

How did you do? (check)

☐ I was able to clearly imagine the pictures.

☐ I was able to imagine some of the pictures.

☐ I couldn't picture any of the pictures.

If you had problems imaging these situations, don't worry. Many people get better at imagery with practice. Also, you may be better at imagining some things than others. Keep practicing and trying different images. See what works for you. Let's start by imagining some peaceful scenes.

The Peaceful Scene

Did you know that you could relax just by picturing yourself somewhere relaxing? Pretend you're at the beach, on vacation, in the mountains, wherever you feel comfortable. This relaxes your mind and helps to switch your nervous system over to COOL mode.

Here are two examples to try. Find a quiet place, take a few deep breaths, close your eyes, and picture these scenes (you can read the scenes aloud into a tape recorder and play it back, if you want to picture the scenes exactly as I wrote them here).

Beach
Picture yourself on a beautiful white, sandy beach. It's a perfect sunny day – warm, but not too hot. Feel the breeze coming in off the ocean. Smell the relaxing scent of the ocean air. Hear the sounds of the waves as they gently break on the shore. Hear the sound of seagulls in the distance. Feel the sand moving between your toes as you walk along the

shore. Look down at the beach as you walk. See the many beautiful sea shells lying on the sand. Go ahead, pick one up. Feel how smooth the shell has become from years of gently rocking in the ocean. Walk down to the water line and let the waves come up over your ankles. Feel the water against your skin as it moves back and forth. Look back up to the beach. There is a comfortable, colorful beach chair that's just waiting for you to sit in. Go ahead. Walk up and sit in the chair. Stare out over the ocean. Look at the big white sail-boats out on the ocean, slowly gliding along. Feel the cool sensation of the sand on your feet and the warmth of the sun on your face. Just sit back and relax. When you are ready, take 5 slow, deep breaths and then gently open your eyes.

Waterfall

You are walking through a beautiful green forest. The weather is perfect. It's cool under the trees, but you are warmed by the rays of the sun, which make their way down through the tops of the trees. You are walking on a soft path. Feel the ground gently give way with each step you take. Smell the pine trees. Look through the trees and see gentle woodland animals dashing about and colorful birds gliding through the air. You hear the sound of rushing water. Walk towards the sound. In a clearing, you can see that the sound is coming from a cool waterfall. The sound gets louder but is becoming more and more peaceful. Feel the droplets of water softly touch your cheek as you get nearer. You see a boulder along the side of the stream right below the waterfall. Go ahead and sit on the boulder. Feel your legs and body relax as you settle down. Take a few minutes to sit there watching the waterfall while you completely relax.

Other Imagery Exercises

There is no limit to the number of things you can imagine that may make you feel relaxed. You can imagine yourself being in any place that is peaceful, comfortable, or relaxing to you. You could also picture an image in your mind of something that is relaxing to you. You can picture yourself floating on a cloud, swimming underneath the waves, or jumping on a rainbow. There is no limit to what you can imagine. Try different images and see what works best for you. Keep track of what works by writing and checking your answers below:

My favorite peaceful scene is: _____.

I am best at imagining: ☐ Sights ☐ Sounds ☐ Smells ☐ Tastes ☐ Touches

A comfortable place where I can sit to use imagery is: _____.

The best time of day for me to use imagery is: _____.

Meditation

Meditation helps you to relax by paying attention to something that is calming and by emptying your mind of all stressful thoughts. Meditation can help you to relax and feel more peaceful throughout the day. Like anything else, it takes practice for it to work well.

There are many different ways to meditate and many things that you can focus on to feel calmer. When you are meditating, try to follow these rules:

❧ Practice regularly. You need to practice at least 10 to 15 minutes a day for meditation to work well. Most people can meditate for longer and longer as they practice.

❧ Find a quiet place to meditate.

❧ Start by taking some slow, deep breaths. This will relax your body while keeping you alert.

❧ Don't be frustrated if you get distracted. This is normal. Just slowly get back into your concentration. You will get better at this as you practice.

Some Forms of Meditation

Let's look at some different kinds of meditation, including focused awareness, mantra, visualization meditation, and walking meditation.

Focused Awareness

Sit quietly in a chair with your eyes closed and allow your mind to gently become aware of what is around you. Hear the sounds around you. Feel the position of your body in your chair. Pay attention to the air temperature and the tiniest breeze against your cheeks. Do not try to control what you pay attention to. Just allow your focus to gently go to whatever is happening around you, even if it is something very small like the sound of a clock ticking. If you are distracted by your thoughts, gently redirect yourself to what is happening around you.

OMMMM

Mantra

A mantra is a word or a phrase that you repeat over and over. You may repeat this word aloud or in your head. The word may be as simple as a single sound. One common mantra is repeating the sound "OM" over and over. A mantra may also be a phrase that makes you feel relaxed (for example, "stay calm") or a prayer that you repeat. The important thing is to focus on your mantra and try not to let other thoughts distract you.

Visualization Meditation

This is kind of like a mantra, but instead of repeating a sound or phrase, you keep focusing your mind on an image. The image can be something as simple as a color, a rainbow, or a cloud. There is no limit to what you can visualize. Just like with the other kinds of meditation, try to stay focused and gently return to your meditation if you are distracted.

Walking Meditation

Walking meditation is similar to focused awareness, except that you are walking instead of sitting. So make sure that YOU KEEP YOUR EYES OPEN for this one. Find a nice, safe place to walk. It can be through a park or along a river (make sure it is safe and make sure others know where you are!!!), or it can be in your own backyard – even your room. As you walk, allow yourself to become aware of your surroundings. Don't try to think too hard about what is happening around you; just gently become aware of things as they happen. Some people find it useful to walk in a certain pattern like a circle; whatever works for you is fine.

Think about how meditation works for you. Try each type of meditation and then answer the following.

The types of meditation that I liked the best were (check):

☐ Focused awareness

☐ Mantra

☐ Visualization meditation

☐ Walking meditation

The types of meditation that I liked the *least* were (check):

☐ Focused awareness

☐ Mantra

☐ Visualization meditation

☐ Walking meditation

Did you have any problems with meditation?   ☐ YES   ☐ NO

If you answered YES, what type of problems did you have?

☐ Couldn't concentrate long enough.   ☐ Couldn't find a quiet place.

☐ Got bored.   ☐ It didn't seem to help.

OTHER: _____

_____

If you had problems, don't worry! Meditation takes lots of practice. Most people get better at meditation with practice, and many find it relaxing. However, no one strategy works the same for everyone. You have to try different things and see what helps you to relax the most. Just make sure that you don't give up on any of the ideas in this book until you've given it a good try (unless it makes you uncomfortable in any way).

Congratulations!

You have earned two more ice blocks.

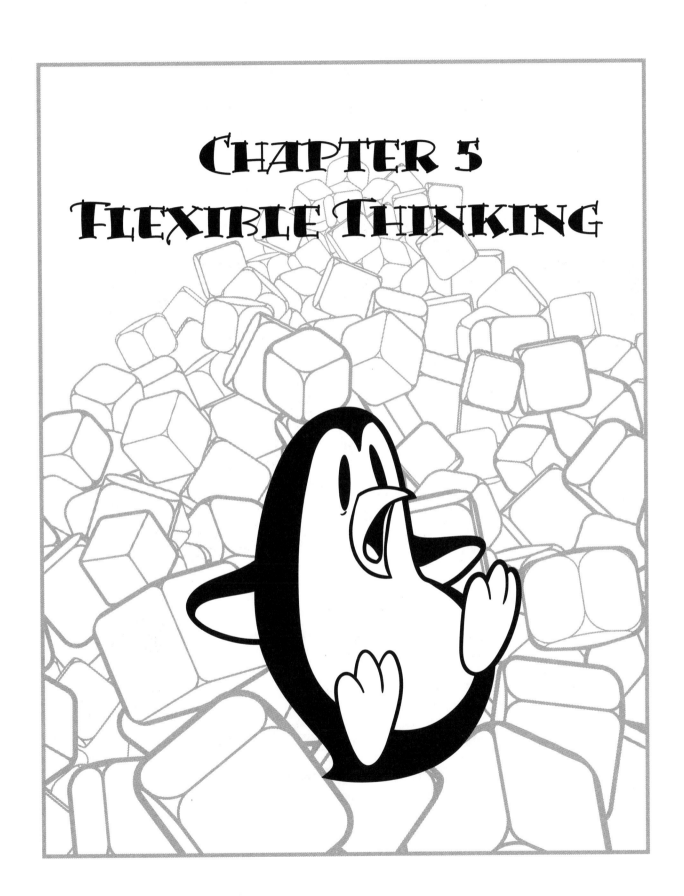

CHAPTER 5
FLEXIBLE THINKING

Something happens to the way we think when we become stressed or nervous. We start to think in ways that are incorrect and that don't make sense.

This may happen to you when you get nervous, frustrated, angry, or even excited. The problem with your thinking when you become upset can usually be described in one word: **inflexible.**

What Exactly Is Inflexible Thinking?

Inflexible thinking means that you see things as being completely one way or the other; all or nothing.

Examples

@ If you get low grade on a test, you may think, I HAVE FAILED **FOREVER**.

@ If you can't find your book bag in the morning, you may think, THIS IS THE **WORST** DAY OF MY LIFE.

@ If some kid teases you on the playground, you may think, **ALL** OF THE KIDS IN THIS SCHOOL ARE BULLIES.

Many kids also think in a way that is known as rigid.

This means that things have to be a certain way for them to be happy: **THE EXACT SAME WAY ... ALL OF THE TIME!!!!!!**

More Examples

@ If your family has pizza on a Friday night, you must ALWAYS have pizza on Friday nights. If you don't – WATCH OUT, MOM AND DAD!!!!

@ You get to school early to go to your chorus rehearsal. When you get there, you find out it has been cancelled – MAJOR PANIC!!!

@ You do homework at the same time, in the same exact order – DON'T TRY TO CHANGE THIS!!!

@ You make your mom drive you to soccer practice the same exact way – DON'T TRY A SHORT-CUT, MOM!!!

@ You must follow the school rules EXACTLY and YOUR CLASSMATES must also follow these rules EXACTLY – if they don't, you HAVE to tell on them.

Flexibility/Inflexibility Quiz

To see how flexible or rigid you are, take this little quiz (there are no right or wrong answers!). Circle the letter of the statement that best describes your reaction.

1. When you come home from school, you realize that you forgot to bring a math worksheet home for homework.

   How do you react?
   a. It wouldn't really bother me that much.
   b. I would get a little upset but then try to come up with a plan for getting the worksheet (for example, get it off the computer or get it from a friend of mine).
   c. I would completely freak out (yell, scream, panic, etc.).

2. You see another kid using a cell phone at school. It's not allowed.

   How do you react?
   a. I don't care what the other kids do.
   b. It would kind of bother me, but I will let the teachers deal with it (but I do know that I need to tell someone if another student is doing something that is dangerous).
   c. I can't believe that kid is breaking the rules!!! I'm going to run and tell on him, immediately!

3. Someone has come into your room and changed some things around without asking your permission first.

   How do you react?
   a. No big deal.
   b. I would get a little upset, but then try to find out who did it and why.
   c. I would yell at everyone in the house and keep yelling until I found out who was responsible for this horrible act!!!

4. It's Saturday morning and you are supposed to have a lacrosse game today. You wake up early, get dressed, and go over to the field. When you get there, you see a big sign that reads, "GAME CANCELED."

   How do you react?
   a. Oh well, at least I'm up and dressed now. Maybe I can practice a little.
   b. I would be disappointed, and it would bother me for the morning, but then I would get over it.
   c. THAT'S IT! My whole weekend is ruined!!! I'm going to quit lacrosse.

71

5. You are expecting your friend to come over on Saturday afternoon. Your friend doesn't make it and doesn't call to tell you. When you see your friend at school on Monday, she explains that she had a party to go to and forgot to tell you. Your friend says she is sorry.

   How do you react?
   a. That's OK. She said she was sorry. No big deal.
   b. I'm a little mad at her, but I'll get over it.
   c. I will never talk to her again!!!

How did you answer?

If most of your answers were the letter "a," you are really easy-going and not rigid at all. However, there may be certain areas in your life that you are rigid about (most people are rigid in at least a few areas of life). Finish the chapter and see if the information is ever useful.

If most of your responses were the letter "b," you usually get a little upset when things don't go your way, but you get over it pretty quickly. Reading this chapter may help you to get over things even quicker.

If most of your responses were the letter "c," you are probably too rigid and inflexible. Unexpected changes make you very upset. READ ON!

Types of Thought Patterns

There are different ways to talk about thought patterns that are too rigid or inflexible. A psychiatrist by the name of Aaron Beck looked very closely at these types of thought processes and called them "cognitive distortions." A psychologist by the name of Albert Ellis looked at them as "irrational beliefs." However you want to say it, these are ways of thinking that just don't make sense when you really think about it.

Let's look at some of these thought processes and think about why they don't make sense.

All-or-Nothing Thinking

Things are completely one way or completely the other way. You can't see any "in-between." For example, if you get a B- on a homework assignment, you think, "That's it! I am a complete failure!"

Why this doesn't make sense:
Things are hardly ever completely one way or the other. There are many "in-betweens" in life, and things often change.

Overgeneralization

If a bad thing happens, you think, "it is going to happen like this ALL THE TIME." For example, you make a mistake at soccer practice and the other team scores. You feel like quitting because you think this is going to happen at ALL of the games.

Why this doesn't make sense:
There is no good reason why something needs to happen ALL THE TIME just because it happened once. It may happen again, but it may not. It is very unusual for something to happen ALL THE TIME. Even the sun will stop shining eventually (don't worry, that is billions of years from now!).

Mental Filter

You only think about the bad things and forget about all of the things that aren't so bad. For example, your friend is late one day and you think, "What a terrible friend for being late!" But you forget about all of the good things that your friend does for you.

Why this doesn't make sense:
Why only think about the bad things? The good things don't go away just because something bad happens. That's like thinking that the good things have magically disappeared. The good things have happened and do happen and will continue to happen. You can't change that just by thinking about the bad things.

Setting off the Avalanche

When something wrong happens (even something small), it is like starting an avalanche. All of a sudden it seems as if your entire world is falling apart. For example, during your first period of the day, you can't find your science assignment and you think, "This is the WORST day ever. EVERYTHING is going wrong!"

Why this doesn't make sense:
You can't just pretend that something doesn't exist any more. Just because something bad happens, it doesn't mean that EVERYTHING bad is happening. It may feel that way, but it isn't true.

The "Should, Have to, and Must" Rule

You set very high standards for yourself and others. It can be good to set high standards for yourself, but your standards are *impossible* and make you nervous. You may also make other people feel uncomfortable. It's like you are always using words like "should," "have to," and "must" with yourself and others.

Examples:

🌀 "I HAVE TO get straight A's, all the time."

🌀 "Other kids SHOULD follow all the rules the same way that I do."

🌀 "I MUST be perfect at my band practices."

Why this doesn't make sense:
NOBODY can live up to super-high standards or goals ALL THE TIME. It just isn't possible. So, take it easy on yourself and others. Everyone makes mistakes sometimes.

The Worry Rule

If something is coming up that is challenging or that you are a bit nervous about, you think that you have to constantly worry about it. For example, you have to give a speech at school in a month and you keep worrying about it over and over again.

Why this doesn't make sense:
Just because you worry, it doesn't mean that things will get better. In fact, you CAN'T make anything better by worrying about it! It would be better to look at the things you are worried about as problems to be solved. This will help to make them less scary.

Believing the Worst

You always think that the very worst is going to happen. For example, before your chorus recital you keep worrying that you will trip on the way up to the stage, your pants will fall down, and the whole school will laugh at you.

Why this doesn't make sense:
How do you know the worst is going to happen? Are you some kind of psychic or fortuneteller? You can't possibly know for certain how things are going to turn out.

Believing in the Perfect Solution

You think that every problem should have a quick and perfect solution. For example, let's say you are having problems with learning a new language. Usually you learn things very quickly, but this is taking a long time to learn. It is making you very frustrated and upset because it is taking too long and it doesn't seem like there is an easy way.

Why this doesn't make sense:
Life's problems are not always like a simple math problem. Sometimes there are more than one way to solve a problem. Sometimes people come up with different solutions to a problem. Sometimes you can't solve problems quickly. This doesn't mean that it is a disaster. Some of the best things in life take a long time and a lot of work.

Examples

Now, let's look at some examples of how our thoughts and beliefs can make us feel either stressed or more relaxed.

The INFLEXIBLE Way

Bob is playing a video game on his computer and he is just about to reach a new level when his battery dies. Let's look at how Bob thinks about this situation:

OH NO! This is the WORST THING EVER!!!! This SHOULD never have happened! Now I'll NEVER be able to reach that level again!

Look at the above list. What styles of thinking was Bob using? (you can list more than one)

_____

_____

_____

How do you think Bob feels? _____

_____

Draw a face in the head above that shows how Bob is feeling.

How do you think Bob may act towards other people in the room? _____

_____

_____

For how long do you think Bob will be upset? _____

_____

The FLEXIBLE Way

Julian is also playing a video game on the computer. He too is just about to get to the next level when the battery dies. Let's look at how Julian thinks about this situation.

> Oh boy. That's stinks! Oh well, it's no big deal. This is a pretty easy game and I'll get back to that level next time. I just have to remember to keep my computer charged next time.

How do you think Julian feels? _____

Draw a face in the head above that shows how Julian is feeling.

How do you think Julian may act towards other people in the room? _____

_____

_____

How long do you think that Julian will be upset for? _____

_____

How is Julian thinking differently from Bob? _____

_____

_____

Let's look at this together.

Julian doesn't LIKE the fact that the computer died. However, he is able to understand that it really isn't the end of the world. This helps Julian to stay calm. By staying calm, Julian is able to problem solve.

Julian understands that he can reach the level pretty easily next time, and he will now remember to keep the computer charged. Bob got so upset that he couldn't think straight. So Bob may not learn from his mistake and the same thing may happen to him again.

Now it's your turn. Let's look at how two people are reacting differently to taking a test. Then you can fill in the thought bubble to describe how they must be thinking to feel that way.

Melinda is taking a social studies test. She usually does well in this class and has gotten good grades. She studied hard for the test and knows the chapters pretty well. However, she is completely FREAKING OUT while taking this test. Draw Melinda's face in the circle to show how she is feeling. Write in the thought bubble what she must be "thinking" to feel this way.

José is also taking a social studies test. He also does well in this class and studied hard last night. He also knows the chapter well. José is calm and confident as he takes the test. Draw José's face in the circle to show how he is feeling. Write in the thought bubble what he must be "thinking" to feel this way.

Now, let's think about how YOU react to situations and how YOU may be able to change this. Think about a situation that got you upset. It could be anything – from losing a video game to failing a test. Just try to make it something that didn't happen too long ago, so that you can remember exactly what you were thinking and how you were feeling.

This is the situation that recently got me upset:

_____

_____

_____

_____

This is what I was *thinking* (write it in the thought bubble):

This is how I was *feeling* (draw a face in the circle, like sad, angry, scared, frustrated):

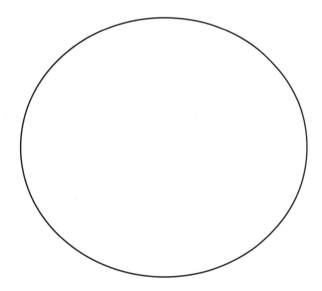

Now, let's look differently at that situation! Try to think different thoughts or look at the situation differently so that you don't feel as upset, sad, frustrated, overwhelmed, or nervous.

This is my NEW and more FLEXIBLE way of looking at that exact same situation:

Now that I have looked at the situation differently, this is how I feel (draw a face in the circle):

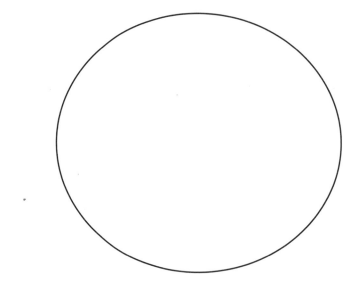

CONGRATULATIONS!!!!

You've discovered that by changing the way you think about a situation, you can change the way that you feel.

Changing the way you think takes a lot of practice. If you keep working at thinking about situations differently, you WILL start to feel better. With time, you will become more flexible and less rigid without having to think about it too much. This will help you feel less anger and stress.

So, now you've learned to calm your body, you've learned to calm your mind, and you've learned to look at situations differently. All of these skills can help you feel less stress when you are faced with problems. This helps you to think more clearly and to solve problems with your intelligence and skills.

In the next chapter we will discuss some ways to use problem solving.

Congratulations!

You have earned two more ice blocks.

CHAPTER 6
PROBLEM SOLVING

Now you are calm. Now you are thinking clearly. It's time to PROBLEM SOLVE!!!

The first step to solving a problem is to decide what the problem really is. This isn't always as easy as it sounds.

A lot of kids become overwhelmed when they are faced with a problem, especially if it is a problem that they haven't dealt with before. When kids are stressed, they may have trouble naming the problem. If asked what the problem is, they may say things like:

🌀 "Everything is falling apart!"

🌀 "I can't take it!"

🌀 "It's too much!"

🌀 "I don't know what the problem is-everything is a problem!"

They are so upset by having a problem – any problem – that they can't even tell what it is that is bothering them.

To help with problem solving, it is useful to start by breaking the problems down into different areas. Let's try it so you can see if this is helpful for you.

SCHOOL	**OTHER KIDS**
Rank:_____	Rank:_____
BROTHERS and/or SISTERS	**PARENTS**
Rank:_____	Rank:_____
ACTIVITIES	**OTHER**
Rank:_____	Rank:_____

Think about the problems that you may have in different areas in your life as shown in the boxes above.

For **School,** think about problems that you may have with some of your classes. Maybe you're not doing well in one or two subjects; maybe you have a big test coming up.

For **Other Kids,** think about problems that you have with other kids. Maybe you think that some kids are picking on you; maybe you are having a problem with making friends; maybe you had an argument with a friend.

For **Parents**, think about any arguments or disagreements that you have had with your parents. Maybe you don't agree with their rules. Maybe your parents don't let you do something that you really want to do.

For **Brothers and Sisters**, think about any fights or disagreements that you have with your brother or sister (if you don't have a brother or sister, think of a cousin, best friend, or other close person).

For **Activities**, think about problems that you may have with the activities you do (sports, chorus, band, chess club, and so on). Maybe you are not doing as well as you'd like in the activity; maybe you are having problem with the coach or teacher.

One box has been left blank (**Other**) in case there is another area of your life that you are having trouble with – maybe your health; maybe you are having problems sleeping; maybe you can't get to a certain level in a computer game. Just fill in the box with a description of the problem area. If you can't think of anything, just leave this box blank.

Now, for the important part. Rank your problem areas by putting them in order from the biggest to the smallest problems. For the area that is the most troubling for you, give it a rank of 1, the area that is the next biggest problem for you, give it a rank of 2, the next area, a 3, and so on.

Take a look at your work. Hopefully, you will see that you don't have major problems all over the place. Sure, there may be one or two areas that are a problem right now, but there are some areas of your life that are actually going pretty well.

Concentrate on the areas that you ranked high for problems. But even within these areas, it may not all be bad. That is why it may help to break down your problem areas even more. For example, you may have some problems with other kids right now, and this may be ranked high on your list. But if you look closer at the area, you may realize that it is really only one or two kids who seem to be the problem. Figuring that out will make it easier for you to focus on what you need to change.

Let's take a closer look at one of the areas above. Let's choose school because that is an area that is very important in your life right now.

Solving Your School Problems

When asked how they feel about school, some kids may say things like:

"School is horrible."

"I hate it!"

"I can't stand it!"

And when they are asked, "What is it about school that you don't like?" they may give a one-word answer:

EVERYTHING!!!

But when they take a close look at the school day, something happens. They find out that not *all* of school is a problem. In fact, they usually discover that it may be only one or two classes that are causing a problem. This helps them to recognize real problems, which they can then find some solutions to. Let's see if this can be helpful for you.

Going over your school day is easy. Just think of your day class by class. On the next page, you can list your periods for the day (eight periods are listed, but you may have more or fewer periods, you can leave periods blank or write in more periods). Then give your classes a ranking. Let's do it like this:

"Like": For classes that you enjoy, are pretty good at, and don't usually have any problems in.

"Don't Like": For classes that you don't enjoy, may not be good at, or that you have problems in.

"So, So": For classes that are in between "Like" and "Don't Like." Maybe you're not super interested in the subject, but you do O.K. and like the teacher. Or maybe you find the teacher to be somewhat strict, but you really enjoy the subject. Or maybe you kind of like the subject, kind of like the teacher, and do O.K. in the class.

My School Day

Write in the name of the class (You can include Lunch and Gym) and circle the rating for that class (Like, Don't Like, So, So)

Period 1	**Class:** _____	Like	Don't Like	So, So
Period 2	**Class:** _____	Like	Don't Like	So, So
Period 3	**Class:** _____	Like	Don't Like	So, So
Period 4	**Class:** _____	Like	Don't Like	So, So
Period 5	**Class:** _____	Like	Don't Like	So, So
Period 6	**Class:** _____	Like	Don't Like	So, So
Period 7	**Class:** _____	Like	Don't Like	So, So
Period 8	**Class:** _____	Like	Don't Like	So, So

Take a look at your ratings. Most kids (even kids who say that they hate school) have different kinds of ratings: Some "Don't Like," some "So, So," and some "Like." This happens a lot. Most kids don't love *all* of their classes, and most kids don't hate *all* of their classes.

Now, take one of the classes that you gave a rating of "Don't Like." Choose the one that gives you the most problems. Take a closer look at that class and see what you can do about it.

The Class That Gives Me the Most Problems

Name of the class: _____

What are the problems with this class? (circle the ones that are true for you)

Work is too hard   The teacher is mean

The kids next to me are distracting   The room is too noisy

I usually don't do well on the tests   We get too much homework

There is too much writing

Other Problems (describe): _____

_____

Next, start by looking at one of those problems. You can look at the example on the next page for help.

The problem that I am going to try to solve for this class is: _____

_____

Now, it's time to brainstorm. This means that you think about different ways to solve the problem. Don't worry too much right now if the ideas are good or bad. Try to come up with at least five solutions.

Solution 1 _____.

Solution 2 _____.

Solution 3 _____.

Solution 4 _____.

Solution 5 _____.

Next, go over your solutions and decide if they may be "effective" solutions or "ineffective" solutions. An **Effective** solution is a solution that solves the problem without hurting anyone and without causing any further problems. An **Ineffective** solution is a solution that doesn't work, hurts people in some way, or creates other problems.

You may have more than one good solution to choose from. That's fine. In fact, you may want to combine solutions or try one before trying another.

My Plan for Solving the Problem: _____

_____

_____

_____

_____

Now, all that's left for you to do is to try it out. Don't give up if your solution doesn't work right away. Sometimes it takes a while to solve a problem.

Example
The problem that I am going to try to solve for this class is: There are 2 kids who sit at my table in science who are really annoying. This makes it hard for me to concentrate.

Possible Solutions:

Solution 1. Tell the kids to shut up!

Solution 2. Ask the kids nicely to be quiet.

Solution 3. Tell the teacher what is happening and ask to be moved.

Solution 4. Try to ignore the kids.

Solution 5. Show the kids what it feels like by screaming.

My Plan for Solving the Problem:

First, I'm going to see if I can just ignore the kids. If that doesn't work, then I will ask them nicely to be quiet. If that doesn't work, I will ask the teacher if I could be moved.

How Do I Come up With Effective Solutions?

Think about these tips when coming up with ways to solve a problem:

1. **Experience** – Use your own experience to solve problems by asking questions like: Has this happened to me before? If so, what helped? What definitively DID NOT help?

2. **Observation** – Watch how others solve the same kind of problem. What do other kids do about this problem? You may think that you are the only one who is having the problem, but if you look carefully, you will probably find that other kids have the same kind of problem.

3. **Advice** – It's perfectly O.K. to ask someone for advice on how to solve a problem. Don't be shy about this. Ask someone that you feel comfortable with, someone you can trust, and someone who you've found helpful before. That person may be a parent, a brother or sister, a friend, a counselor, a teacher, and so on.

4. **Thinking It Through** – If you are worried about your solution, you can run through it in your mind. Think about the good things that may happen if you try your solution and then think about anything bad that may happen. If there are a lot of good things that can happen and no really bad things, then go for it! However, if there is a *real* chance that something bad may happen, then you want to try another solution.

5. **Experiment** – If there is no real danger (see below) of something bad happening from your solution, go ahead and try it. See what happens. You may find that you need to change your solution a little or you may need to try something else.

Important Note on Problem Solving!

When NOT to do problem solving on your own:
If a situation is in any way dangerous, do not try to solve the problem on your own. Get help, immediately. Also, don't try to problem solve on your own if one of your solutions might cause some kind of harm or get you in trouble.

Examples of times to get help:
- Somebody is bullying you
- Another kid asks you to do something that is against the rules, or worse yet, the law
- A stranger approaches you outside of the school
- You are feeling very sad and don't know what to do about it
- You are feeling so angry that you think you may try to hurt someone

If you are not sure about whether something is dangerous or not, get help!

Congratulations!

You have earned two more ice blocks.

CHAPTER 7
GETTING ORGANIZED

Becoming more organized can help to reduce stress. But, be careful! Being more organized doesn't mean that you should make a whole bunch of lists or spend hours each day cleaning up your room (although your parents may love that!).

To help with stress, we are going to work on three things in this chapter:

1. How to organize your things so that you don't lose or forget them. Forgetting things like books, assignments, and important papers can be very stressful.

2. How to tell the difference between what is most important to do and what is less important to do. Many people get stressed out by trying to do everything at once.

3. How to manage the way that you use your time. This will help you to finish important things on time (while still finding time to relax and have some fun).

Let's get started.

Organize Your Things and Your Work

Answer these questions by circling the answer that fits you:

1. What does your room look like?
    a. It looks like a tornado just went through it.
    b. It usually looks nice and neat but not always.
    c. It's so neat and clean that you can eat off of the floor.

2. What does your desk at school look like?
    a. It's so messy that there could be an elephant in there and you wouldn't know.
    b. Not bad. I can usually find what I want.
    c. It's neater than the teacher's desk.

3. How are you with writing down homework assignments?
    a. I forget at least once a week.
    b. I hardly ever forget to write down an assignment but it does happen once in awhile.
    c. I write down all of my assignments and then rewrite them in alphabetical order.

4. How is your backpack for school?
    a. I'm afraid to open it – I think I heard something growling in there.
    b. Things get a little mixed up, but I can quickly find them.
    c. I place everything in my backpack the same exact way every day.

How did you answer? If most of your answers were "a," you can be quite messy. This can make you stressed when you can't find what you want. This chapter is great for you.

If most of your answers were "c," you are way too organized. Although this may seem like the right way to be, it can make you stressed because you may freak out if things get out of place. No matter how hard you try, things will get out of place once in a while. By reading this chapter, you will learn that organization can be helpful but trying to be perfect all the time can only make your stress worse.

If most of your answers were "b," you are usually pretty organized but not always. When reading this chapter, try to concentrate on those areas that you think you may need a little help with.

How to Organize Your Things

There are three tips for organizing your things.

First, think about a system that will work for you. Make sure that the things you need the most are the easiest to find. Make sure that you can always reach your pens and pencils. Make sure that your assignment book is close by. If you use an alarm clock, keep it by your bed. Write some other ideas now.

One way that I can better organize my things is: _____

_____

Second, BE CONSISTENT. This is very important. Don't keep changing where you put things, otherwise you will always be losing them. For example, if you keep your calculator in the front pocket of your backpack, then put it back in the front pocket of your backpack when you are done using it. Write down your ideas.

This is where I should always keep my backpack: _____ .

This is where I should always keep my pens and pencils: _____ .

This is where I should always put my homework when finished: _____ .

This is where I should keep my important equipment for my sport or hobby. (Think about one of your sports or hobbies that you have important equipment for: for example, a ball for a sport, musical instrument, karate uniform): _____ .

Third, be prepared to spend SOME time just straightening things up. You don't need to spend all day organizing things. But, *every day* you will need to spend some time organizing your desk, *every day* you will need to clear out and then repack your backpack, and *every day* you will need to spend some time cleaning up your room (sorry)!

Amount of time I should spend on organizing my work things after school:_____ .

Amount of time I should spend on cleaning and organizing my bedroom on the weekends:

_____ .

How to Organize Your Work

Poor organization can make schoolwork hard in a lot of ways. For example:

@ You may have great ideas, but you may have difficulty writing them down on paper in an organized way that gets your ideas across.

@ You may be good at math, but you may get confused when there are a lot of problems on the page.

@ You listen really well in class, but don't do well on the test because you didn't know how to study.

Here are some ideas on how to organize your work.

Use Strategies for Organizing Your Work
Some examples include:

@ Make outlines to organize your writing.

@ Use a highlighter (if you own the book) to mark important information.

@ Use a ruler to keep your math work straight.

@ Use study outlines for tests.

Ask for Help
We all need help with things. A lot of kids need help with organizing their work. Don't be afraid to ask. Your teachers understand that you are a good student and will help you to do as well as you can in class. If you get extra help at school (for example, resource room, study class, extra teachers in class, or aide), ask the people who support you for help with organizing your work. Also, make your parents aware so that they can make sure that you are getting the right help at school.

Learn in Different Ways
One of the best ways to learn is by using information in fun and interesting ways. Try to learn by doing creative activities that get you involved with what you are learning. For example, to help with learning measurements measure your favorite items around the house and compare them. To learn about the Civil War, have big pretend battles in your backyard (safely!). If you like art, then you can draw, color, and paint to help you learn. If you like music, write a song that helps you to remember facts or ideas.

There is no end to the number of activities you can do to make learning fun.

Prioritizing

Many kids think that everything they need to do is super important. This can cause a lot of stress because you feel that you HAVE to do EVERYTHING at ONCE.

But that is just not true! Sure, things have to be done, but everything is not equally important. Figuring out what is more important and what is less important is known as "prioritizing" (pry-o-ri-tize-ing).

To prioritize means that you do what needs to be done first before starting something else.

How Do We Prioritize?
Think about the task you need to do and ask yourself these three questions:
1. How important is it?
2. When does it have to be done?
3. How much time will it take me to finish?

Rank priority in one of three ways:

🌀 Low priority

🌀 Medium priority

🌀 High priority

If something is …

🌀 Really important,

🌀 Due tomorrow, and

🌀 Will take you hours to do …

… that is definitely a HIGH priority. You have to do it NOW.

If something is …

🌀 Not too important,

🌀 Is not due for a month, and

🌀 Will probably take about 20 minutes to finish …

… that is definitely a LOW priority. Unless you're not very busy right now, you are probably better off doing something else first.

There are a lot of times when it is not clear what kind of a priority something is. Just remember to think of the three questions above.

Let's say you have a big, important project to do, but it is not due for a month. That would probably be a medium priority. With this kind of task, you are better off starting it and doing a little each day so that you can finish it on time.

Let's say you have a spelling quiz tomorrow. Even though a quiz may not be as important as a big test, you still want to do well on it, and because it is taking place tomorrow that makes it a high priority.

Now it's your turn to practice: Rank the following tasks by their priority (circle one):

1. You have to memorize a new song for your band recital that is coming up in three months.
    Low Priority   Medium Priority   High Priority

2. You have to write a paragraph on an article you read in class. It's due tomorrow.
    Low Priority   Medium Priority   High Priority

3. You have plenty of sharp pencils, but there are some unsharpened pencils lying in your desk. How much of a priority is it to sharpen these pencils?
    Low Priority   Medium Priority   High Priority

Now it's time to think about your own life. Try to list three things in your life RIGHT NOW for each priority level.

Low Priority

1. _____

2. _____

3. _____

Medium Priority

1. _____

2. _____

3. _____

High Priority

1. _____

2. _____

3. _____

It's not always easy to prioritize, but when you do, it will definitely help to reduce your stress. Just remember to leave time for fun, rest, and relaxation.

Time Management

Guessing how much time it will take to finish something can be tricky, but being good at this can help with stress. Think about these two situations:

🌀 You have a big homework assignment due tomorrow. Without realizing how long it will take to finish, you start the assignment 15 minutes before your bedtime. However, the assignment is taking much longer than you thought. You are tired; your parents are tired. Everybody is now upset, and you are missing your sleep. THIS IS STRESSFUL!

🌀 You have a baseball game to go to today. Your parents are busy working in the yard and remind you an hour ahead of time to start getting dressed. You start playing video games and let time slip by. It is now 5 minutes before you have to leave. Your parents come in from the yard and say, "Oh no! You haven't even STARTED to get dressed!" I don't have to tell you what happens next: Your parents are rushing you; you start yelling; they start yelling, and everybody is STRESSED.

So, how can you get better at managing time?

Ways to Get Better at Managing Time

Practice
Try to estimate how much time it will take you to do something. For example, you can guess how long it will take for you to complete a sheet of math homework, or how long it will take for you to get dressed. Write it down and check your answer. If you were way off, try again. The more you do this, the better your guesses will become.

Use a Clock
That's what clocks are there for! Look at the clock. What time is it now? What do you have to do before the day ends? What time should you start?

Set Alarms
You can set your alarm clock to go off to remind you to start something. These days, there are many devices that can set off alarms, wrist watches, laptops, phones, electronic organizers, hand-held computer gadgets, etc.

Make a List
Make a list of what you need to do before the end of the day and set a time for starting each task. Try to be realistic about how long it will take to do each thing, and don't forget to leave some time free for rest and relaxation.

Get Advice

It is O.K. to ask someone you trust (like a teacher or parent) for help on how to manage your time. You can also ask one of your parents to remind you when you need to start something. But remember: If you ask for help, don't get upset when someone reminds you to start something!

Watch out for "Procrastination" (pro-crass-tin-nay-shun)

Procrastination means we put off doing what we should be doing. We especially put off doing things that are difficult. In fact, people are good at finding the silliest things to do instead of doing something difficult. For example, let's say you have to finish a big writing assignment – TONIGHT – and you haven't even started. The smart thing to do would be to start the assignment – NOW. But suddenly you decide it is time to put all of your baseball cards in alphabetical order. In fact, you may spend hours finding little things to do – anything but what you really need to do.

Keep Balance in Your Life

Nobody can do all the things they want to do. There are so many activities that it is hard to choose just one or two. However, it is important to avoid having too many activities in your schedule. Think about how stressed you will become if you have a big test tomorrow but before studying you have to go to computer club, then karate class, then basketball practice, then practice for your dance and band recitals, and then memorize words for the upcoming spelling bee. Unless you can easily fit everything into your day, you are probably better off doing a few activities that you really enjoy than trying to do everything.

Congratulations!

You have earned two more ice blocks.

What does health have to do with stress? A LOT!!!

Remember what you learned in Chapter 2 about stress and the body. They are connected. Changes in our minds create changes in our bodies, and changes in our bodies can create changes in our minds.

A healthy body can help you to focus better, think more clearly, and deal with problems better. These are all things that can help an awful lot with stress. So, what does it mean to be healthy? We are going to cover four areas in this chapter: nutrition, exercise, sleep, and physical health.

Nutrition

Nutrition has to do with the foods that we eat and the good stuff that our bodies get from these foods. But before we get going, we need to go over a couple of important points:

1. This section has nothing to do with losing weight (if you are very concerned about losing weight, you need to talk to an adult about it).

2. This section will not tell you what you can and can't eat. The point is to help you to choose healthy foods that make you feel good. Do NOT eat anything that may cause you an allergic reaction and check with your parents and doctor before making any big changes in the foods that you eat.

Let's start by looking at some basic ideas about healthy eating.

Eat a Variety of Foods

Scientists place foods into different groups. Foods that can be healthy are often placed into the following groups:

@ Grains (for example, bread and pasta)

@ Vegetables (for example, carrots and lettuce)

@ Fruits (for example, apples and bananas)

@ Dairy (this includes things made from milk like cheese and yogurt)

@ Proteins (things like chicken, fish, and baked beans)

Our body benefits from eating foods from these groups, but you want to have a balance. It's not healthy to eat just one type of food.

Eat Fruits and Vegetables

Fruits and vegetables provide us with vitamins and minerals. These help to keep us healthy. How much of these your body needs depends upon things like your age, height, and weight.

Stay Away From too Much Caffeine

Caffeine can kick your nervous system into HOT mode. As you will remember from Chapter 2, our nervous system's HOT mode gets our body ready for action. Caffeine can get the nervous system really excited. This can make you feel nervous, stressed, and jumpy. That is not good for your body or your mind. Be careful! Caffeine is not just in coffee. It is also in power drinks (the kind that promise to keep you alert and active), tea, most sodas, and even chocolate.

Stay Away From too Much Sugar

Too much sugar can be bad for your health. It can also affect your blood-sugar levels. This can change the way you feel. Blood sugar can be too low or too high. This can make you feel tired, confused, nervous, shaky, jumpy, and a lot of other things. Any of these symptoms should be reported to an adult immediately!

Stay Away From too Much Junk Food

Junk food is food that does very little good for your body. Super sugary candy, food that is almost all fat, and food that is made from mostly artificial ingredients are all examples of this kind of food. Sometimes people eat more of these foods when they are feeling stressed. Eating this type of food may make you feel good while you are eating it, but soon after your body can start to feel empty and tired. This is not good for managing stress or for your health.

Most people need to change the things that they eat at least a little. What about you?

One food (or type of food) that I should be eating or drinking *more* of is (check):

☐ Fruits (for vitamins)   ☐ Vegetables (for vitamins)   ☐ Dairy (to build strong bones)

☐ Proteins (for energy and muscle growth)   ☐ Grains (for energy)

One food (or type of food) that I should be eating or drinking *less* of is:

☐ Soda or power drinks (too much caffeine)   ☐ Candy (too much sugar)

☐ Fast food (too much fat and artificial ingredients; not good for my body)

☐ Other: _____

The Way You Eat

It's not just WHAT you eat that can change your health and stress levels. The WAY that you eat can also make a difference.

Let's start with a true/false quiz.

True/False Quiz

(Circle the correct answer)

I never eat a big breakfast.	True	False
I sometimes eat while walking or standing.	True	False
I like to eat right before I go to bed.	True	False
I sometimes eat way too much.	True	False
I usually eat while watching television.	True	False
I like to eat fast.	True	False

If any of your answers were "True," you probably need to change one or more of your eating habits. Let's take a look at some ideas of healthy eating. Since you don't have control over all these things, talk to your parents about them.

Eat MORE SLOWLY

You will enjoy your food more when you take the time to taste it. This means eating more slowly. Chewing your food can help. Sometimes people "shovel" food into their mouths like it is an Olympic sport. When you don't chew enough, you don't get all of the good stuff that you can from your food. Also, you can't really taste your food when you eat too fast; besides, eating too fast can give you a stomachache.

Sit Down When You Eat

When you sit down to eat, it helps you to enjoy your food and to make healthier eating choices. It may seem easy to pick up a piece of junk food and slam it in your mouth as you run out of the door. However, if you sat down with the junk food, really looked at it, really thought about it, you might decide that you want something healthier.

Choose a Relaxing Place to Eat

It's not a good idea to eat while watching television or playing video games. Kids are usually so distracted by what they are watching or playing that they don't really taste their food or think about whether or not their food is healthy. Sit down at the dinner table if you are home. At school, sit down at a lunch table. Try not to eat and do something else at the same time whenever you can.

Choose a Good Time to Eat

Try to eat only when you are hungry. Many people eat because they are bored or stressed. This type of eating isn't healthy, and at many of these times people are choosing unhealthy foods to eat. Also, try not to eat a lot of food too close to bedtime. This can make it hard for your body to digest and can make it hard to sleep well.

Eat a Good Breakfast

You've probably heard this before, but it's good advice. Breakfast gives your body the fuel it needs to get through the morning. It also helps to start up your digestive system, which helps your body to digest food better throughout the day.

Now, make a plan for change. Start with one small change. Before you know it you will be eating healthier and feeling better.

One Small Change That I'm Going to Start With
(Check)

☐ I'm not going to eat a lot before bedtime.   ☐ I'm going to eat slower.

☐ I'm going to really try to taste my food.   ☐ I'm going to sit down to eat.

☐ I'm not going to eat while watching TV.   ☐ I'm going to eat a better breakfast.

Exercise

What does exercise have to do with stress? A lot! Exercise can relax your muscles, help you to breathe better, help you to think more clearly, help you to sleep better, and generally make you feel good.

All of these good things about exercise can help to reduce stress. So it is a good idea to start exercising regularly (if you are not already). However, it can be hard to start and stick with an exercise program. These steps can help.

Step 1. Decide What You Would Like to Do

There are many fun ways to get exercise. You can exercise in a group or you can do it alone. You can do exercises that help your muscles to get stronger, you can do exercises that help your lungs and heart to work better, and you can do exercises that help all of these areas. You can do exercises outside, or inside, or both. You can do exercises that you need equipment for or exercises that only require your own body. Just make sure that you don't do anything your doctor won't allow and don't do anything that hurts.

The Exercise (or exercises) I would like to do is: _____.

Step 2. Pick a Time to Do It

This is important. Picking a time will help you to get started and to stick with your plan. Pick a time that you know you can stick with. During the school year, it may be good to exercise right after school or after you have eaten dinner (and given your stomach time to digest your food). Of course, you will have to do your exercise at a time that is safe (for example, don't go for a run late at night).

If you exercise as part of a team, your exercise time has been made for you (for example, you may have basketball practice three times a week at 7 p.m.). However, you may want to exercise on your own on the days that you have off from practice.

The time that I am going to do my exercise is: _____.

Step 3. Start Small

If you try to do too much when you begin, you are going to get tired and sore. This will make you want to quit. Exercise should make you feel good, not bad. It should take some effort, but it should not hurt or make you so sore and tired that you don't want to do it again.

I am going to start by doing _____ minutes of exercise each time.

Step 4. Build Slowly

Try to do a little more exercise each time that you train. If you exercise regularly, you will feel better and better. When you feel better, it will be time to try to do some more. Your body needs to be challenged to grow stronger. If you do the same amount of exercise each day, your body won't be challenged and you won't get the best results from your exercise. After you get started, fill in the following.

When I _____**, I will do a little more.**

Step 5. Mix It Up

Your body quickly gets used to things. If you keep doing the same exercise and the same amount of exercise, your body will get used to this and stop growing healthier. This is why it is important to change your exercise once in a while.

There are many ways that you can change your exercise routine. You can do the same exercise a little bit differently. For example, if you always run on a track, try running on grass or on the beach.

There are also many ways that you can change how you get the same total amount of exercise. For example, let's say that you like to do 30 pushups. One day, you can do 5 pushups in a row for 6 times (5 X 6 = 30), or you can do 10 pushups 3 times in a row (10 X 3 = 30), or (once you have gotten stronger) you can do 30 pushups in a row (30 X 1 = 30).

You can also try some of the video game systems that encourage you to move. These systems have a lot of exciting games that you can choose from that get you to do many different types of exercises.

You can also do completely different exercises from time to time. Many athletes do this; it's called cross-training. For example, swimmers may run. Runners may swim. Baseball players may lift weights. The important thing is that you are challenging your body by doing things a bit differently. After you get started, fill in the following.

To change my routine, I will _____**.**

Sleep

Have you ever had to get up when you felt really tired and all you wanted to do was crawl back into bed? How did you feel when you got up? How did you feel for the rest of the day? Were you nice or grouchy? Were you able to pay attention or did you find it hard to focus?

If you're like most kids, you probably don't feel great when you don't get enough sleep. Sleep is really important for your body, your mind, and your feelings. Your body does a lot of work while you sleep. It helps to repair and build muscles; it helps you to organize your thoughts and memory; and it helps you to rest so that you can get through the next day. When you don't sleep well, all kinds of things can happen: You may not be able to move as fast, you may not be able to concentrate, you may not be able to do challenging work, you may be grouchy, you may feel more nervous, and you may not be able to solve problems well.

Different Types of Sleep Problems

There are different kinds of sleep problems. All of them can stop you from getting a full night's sleep. Check off the ones that you have had (at any time in your life).

Sleep Problems

☐ Problems falling asleep

☐ Waking up too early

☐ Sleepwalking

☐ Nightmares

☐ Go to bed too late

☐ Falling asleep on the couch

☐ Falling asleep while watching TV

☐ Waking up during the night

Most people have a bad night's sleep once in a while. This is normal. However, it can become a problem if you have trouble sleeping most of the time or even if you have trouble sleeping a couple of days each week.

How Can You Tell If You're Not Getting Enough Sleep?

Here are a few clues:

❷ You don't want to wake up most mornings.

❷ You are very grouchy in the morning.

❷ You are tired during the day.

❷ You fall asleep during the day when you don't want to (for example, while riding in the back of the car).

❷ You can't concentrate well.

❷ You feel tired.

❷ You yawn a lot.

How Can You Improve Your Sleep?

Make Sure You Get Enough Sleep
Although it may sound like a lot, most kids need around 10 hours of sleep each night. (Some kids may need a little more and some may need a little less, but this is a good number to start with.) So make sure you allow time for these 10 hours. That means if you wake up at 7 a.m., you need to be asleep around 9 p.m. If you wake up earlier, you need to get to bed earlier.

Stick to a Sleep Routine
Try to do the same thing every night before bedtime (you can change this a little on the weekends). That means doing something to get your body and brain ready for bed. For example, if you go to bed at 9 p.m., you may like to watch TV from 8 to 8:30 p.m., then brush your teeth, and then read a little before going to bed at 9 p.m. Some people like to take a bath before bed; some like to listen to relaxing music; some like to have a small, healthy snack at night (but not right before bedtime). Whatever it is that you like to do, just make sure you do it pretty much the same way each night.

Avoid Caffeine and Other Foods/Drinks That Can Rev You Up
Eating too much right before bed can make it hard for your body to digest food. Not only is this unhealthy, but you may get a stomachache, and this will keep you up. Drinking too much before bed will make you have to get up in the middle of the night to go to the bathroom. Drinking drinks that have caffeine in them before bedtime is definitely not a good idea. Not only will you have to go to the bathroom, but the caffeine will keep you awake.

Exercise Regularly (But Not Right Before Bed)
Exercising will help your body to relax. Just be careful not to do a whole bunch of exercise right before bed. This will make it hard for you to relax your brain and body.

Don't Try to FORCE Yourself to Sleep
Sleep should happen naturally. If you follow a routine and take the advice above, you should be asleep within about 10 minutes after going to bed. If you find yourself awake, don't panic and don't TRY to sleep. Just try to relax and clear your mind. One night of bad sleep isn't going to be very harmful, so just relax and let your brain and body take over.

Remember Your Relaxation Exercises
These can help with sleep. The more relaxed you are, the better you will sleep. You can do relaxation exercises at night to help with sleep but don't do them right before bedtime. You have to focus and think when doing relaxation exercises, and you may be too tired to do them properly if you are just about ready to fall asleep.

Physical Health

Your physical health is very important. It can be very stressful to be sick or not feel well. Each person's physical health is different, and it is important to know about any problems that you may have with your health. Even if you are already healthy, you still need to be aware of things to do to keep your body that way.

Special Conditions

Some kids have special conditions that need extra attention, like diabetes or asthma. If that is the case for you, it is important to listen to the advice of your doctor and parents about what you have to do to take care of your condition.

To get an idea of your physical health and what you need to do, check and write your answers below.

☐ I do not have a special medical condition.

☐ I do have a special medical condition it is: _____

These are some of the things that I need to do to take care of my condition:

1. _____

2. _____

3. _____

4. _____

Allergies
Some kids have allergies and must be careful to stay away from the things that they are allergic to. Check and write below if you have allergies and, if so, what to do to take care of yourself.

☐ I do not have any allergies (check with your parents if you are unsure).

☐ I am allergic to: _____

This is what I need to do to avoid the things that I am allergic to: _____

_____

_____

Infections

Nobody likes to get sick. Luckily, there are a lot of things we can do to avoid getting sick. Some of these things include:

- Washing hands (especially before eating and after being in a place with a lot of people)

- Staying away from people who are sick

- Keeping hands away from mouth, nose, and eyes (you can catch a cold by rubbing your eyes with the cold virus!)

- Only eating food that is clean and safely prepared

- Being careful about sharing food with others

Also, if you are doing the other healthy things we talked about in this chapter (eating right, getting sleep, exercising), your body will be better able to fight off germs.

Congratulations!

You have earned two more ice blocks.

CHAPTER 9
GETTING ALONG WITH OTHER KIDS

Getting along with others can also help to reduce your stress levels. Think about how stressed you may feel when these things happen:

@ You get into an argument with your best friend and she says that she doesn't want to come over to your house any more.

@ You are invited to a party where you don't know a lot of the other kids.

@ They change your lunch period and you don't have anybody to sit with.

@ You don't like the games that the other kids play at recess, so you stand around alone until the bell rings.

@ Some kids on the bus are calling you mean names.

All of these situations can be stressful. But there are a lot of different ways that you can make them better. By learning some ways of getting along with others, you will feel a lot less stressed. In this chapter, we will look at three areas:

1. Meeting New People

2. Making Friends

3. Dealing With Bullies

Meeting New People

How do you feel when you have to meet new people? (check)

☐ I love it. It doesn't bother me at all.

☐ I get a little nervous, but once I meet them I feel better.

☐ I get really nervous and don't like to do it.

☐ I get absolutely terrified!!!

If you get nervous about meeting new people, don't worry! A lot of kids (and many adults) get nervous when meeting new people.

The key is to try to find some way to relax, at least a little, so that you are not terrified when meeting new people. This is the time when you can try any of the skills that you have learned throughout this book.

Chapter 9: Getting Along With Other Kids

1. Think about how you can relax your body before you meet someone.

   List at least two things that you can do to relax your body before you meet someone (if you need a reminder, go back over Chapter 3):

   _____

   _____

   _____

2. Think about how you can relax your mind before you meet someone.

   List at least two things that you can do to relax your mind before you meet someone (if you need a reminder, go back over Chapter 4):

   _____

   _____

   _____

3. Remember what you learned about flexible thinking in Chapter 5. If you think calm and confident thoughts, you are going to feel calmer and more confident. If you think scary thoughts then you are going to feel afraid and not very confident when meeting someone.

   Take a look at some of the kinds of thoughts that make kids feel nervous before they meet someone. Try to change those thoughts to a better way of thinking by writing on the lines below.

   Negative Thought: "Nobody is going to like me."

   Positive Thought: _____.

   Negative Thought: "I'm going to do something really embarrassing."

   Positive Thought: _____.

   Negative Thought: "I'm not going to have any fun."

   Positive Thought: _____.

   Negative Thought: "I don't know what to do or say."

   Positive Thought: _____.

Say the negative thought out loud **and** then say the positive thought out loud. Notice how each sounds and notice how each one makes you feel.

If you are nervous about meeting new people, you can feel better by repeating the positive thoughts (in your head!). This will help you to feel calmer and more confident. However, don't worry if you feel a little bit nervous when you are meeting someone for the first time. Many kids (and adults) feel this way. **The important thing is to keep at it and try to have fun.**

Making Friends

Some kids get stressed out about making friends. This may be because they feel that they do not know how to make friends or they may feel that they should have a lot more friends than they do. Also, sometimes parents, teachers, or counselors may be telling you that you should make more friends and this can make you feel nervous.

Here are some ways to feel better about making friends.

1. Don't make a super, duper big deal about it. This will only make you nervous and then you may be too shy to try to make friends. Try to have fun and don't worry too much if you try to make a new friend and it doesn't work out.

2. Make it as easy as possible. To do this we are going to take another look at your social circle on page 16.

Take a look at the circle that says "My Acquaintances." These are the kids that you may be able to move into your "Friends" circle.

> ***To Review:*** *An acquaintance is someone that you probably know by name and probably see in the same kind of place on a regular basis. For example, these may be kids who share a hobby or sport with you (in your karate class, in the same scout troop, in band or chorus with you, and so on). These kids already know you at least a little so you are not a complete stranger to them. However, you are not quite friends either.*

Make a list of the kids in your acquaintances circle who you think are nice. It's no use trying to make friends with someone if you feel that they are mean or ignore you.

Acquaintances who I think are nice (write their names):

1. _____

2. _____

3. _____

4. _____

5. _____

One great way to make friends is to find kids who have things in common with you. This means they like some of the same things that you do. This makes it easier to talk about things and can make it easier to have a play date if you know what you both like to do.

Think of acquaintances from your list that you may have something in common with. If you are unsure, it is O.K. to ask. For example, let's say you like a sports team called the Dragons. You can ask the acquaintance, "Do you like the Dragons?" or "Did you see the Dragons game last night?"

List the acquaintance, along with what you have in common with him or her below.

NAME	WHAT WE HAVE IN COMMON

Remember: *You do not have to have EVERYTHING in common with your friends. There will be some things that your friends like that you don't like and some things that you like that your friends don't like. This is perfectly fine!*

Now that you have discovered some acquaintances who may make good friends, you need to come up with a plan for trying it out.

Start with one acquaintance from your list. Look at the example below for help.

Name of acquaintance: _____.

The place (or places) where I usually see this acquaintance:_____.

The time when it will usually be O.K. to start to talk to this acquaintance: _____.

What I can say to this acquaintance that might help us to become friends: _____

_____

_____.

Example

Name of acquaintance: <u>Susan</u>

The place (or places) where I usually see this acquaintance: <u>Sits by me at lunch</u>

The time when it will usually be O.K. to start to talk to this acquaintance: <u>After she</u>

<u>finishes eating</u>

What I can say to this acquaintance that might help us to become friends: <u>"Hi Susan.</u>

<u>I know that you like to go ice skating. I am going ice skating this</u>

<u>weekend with my family. Would you like to come with us?"</u>

These are the sort of things that you need to do to get more kids into your "Friends" circles. It is not important to have a whole bunch of friends. But it can help a lot to have friends to do fun things with and to be there for you when you need help with something.

Dealing With Bullies

You hear a lot of talk about bullying, but what does it really mean? In the following list, check off the things that you think are bullying.

Bullying Is ...

☐ Calling someone names

☐ Tripping someone in the hallway

☐ Saying bad things about somebody

☐ Sending an embarrassing picture of someone over the Internet without their permission

☐ Making somebody feeling left out on purpose

The truth is that any of these things can be bullying. Bullying is something that somebody does to hurt another person's feelings on purpose.

Have you ever been bullied? (check)   ☐ YES   ☐ NO

If you have, don't feel bad. Many kids are bullied at some time or another. This does not mean that there is something bad about you or that you did anything wrong.

The kinds of bullying that have happened to me are (check):

☐ Kids calling me names   ☐ Kids hurting me

☐ Kids leaving me out   ☐ Kids saying bad things about me

☐ Kids sending me mean emails or text messages

☐ Other: _____

Being bullied, or even being afraid of being bullied, can cause a lot of stress. So, it is very important to have a plan for dealing with bullies.

There are four important things that you can do if you feel that you are being bullied.

1. **Report the bullying to your parents, teachers, and other adults that you trust.**

    This is the very first thing that you should do if you feel that you are being bullied. Do not think that the bullies will just stop. Usually, bullies won't stop unless adults make them. Don't be embarrassed to tell someone. Adults are there to help you stay safe. They want to know if somebody is bothering you.

Besides my parents, three people I can report bullying to are (write their names)

_____, _____, and _____.

2. Keep away from bullies whenever possible.

You may not always be able to avoid bullies and certainly shouldn't stop doing what you want to do. However, it is a good idea to avoid bullies when you can. Try to stay around kids who you know are nice. For example, sit with nice kids at lunch, play with nice kids at recess, and talk to nice kids before and after school.

Places where I can find some nice kids and stay away from kids who are mean (check):

☐ Playground ☐ Lunch Room ☐ After-School Activities

☐ In the Classroom ☐ On the Bus ☐ Other: _____

3. If you think it is safe, tell the bully to stop.

Do not fight a bully and don't go up to bullies if you think they are dangerous. However, if it feels safe, you can tell a bully that you don't like what he is doing and ask him to stop in a strong voice. This will show the bully that you are not going to let him keep doing what he is doing.

Remember: Bullies want a reaction from you. If you scream, yell, cry, or try to hit a bully, that will make him feel good. When you do talk to a bully, do it in a way that shows the bully that he is not "getting" to you as much as he wants.

Here are some things I can say to a bully if it feels safe (write your ideas):

_____

_____

_____

4. Be around other kids during times when bullies are around.

Bullies often pick on kids when they are alone. Sometimes bullies will not pick on you if you are around your friends (especially if these friends will stick up for you). So it is important to be around other friends during times when a bully is around. Even if you can't find a friend, try to talk and play with some kids that you think are nice.

Some kids I can sit with, talk to, or play with **during lunch** are (write their names):

_____

_____

_____

Some kids I can sit with, talk to, or play with **during recess** are (write their names):

_____

_____

_____

Some kids I can sit with, talk to, or play with **before the bell rings** are (write their names):

_____

_____

_____

Cyber-Bullying

Cyber-bullying is bullying that happens over the Internet or through other electronic ways, like phones or other kinds of devices. This type of bullying can be just as hurtful as other kinds of bullying.

Have you ever been cyber-bullied? (check and write your answers)

☐ YES   ☐ NO

If YES, describe what happened: _____

_____

What did you do about it?: _____

_____

_____

It is very important to report this kind of bullying to your parents. You can also report this kind of bullying to a trusted adult at school if the bullying happens at school or if it comes from a kid at school. Also, if you are bullied on a website, there may be a place on the website where you can report it. The important thing is to keep track of what happened and report it to your parents. DO NOT talk back to the bully online. This only shows the bully that they have bothered you and they will probably keep doing it.

Congratulations!

You have earned two more ice blocks.

CHAPTER 10
USING MY STRENGTHS

It may seem that people are always trying to teach you things – how to make friends, how to improve at school, how to make eye contact, how to talk to other kids, how to eat more foods, how to pay attention better, how to write better, and so on.

People are trying to teach you things so that you can learn important skills in life. However, all of this help may make you forget the things that you are *good* at.

What does this have to do with stress? A lot!

Feeling good about yourself can make a big difference in your life. Feeling good can help you to better deal with your problems. Also, you usually feel less stress when you are doing things that you are good at.

Everybody has things that they are good at and things that they are not so good at. That's just the way life is. Nobody is good at everything. Think of these examples:

@ Somebody is a great baseball player, but he is not good at drawing.

@ Somebody is great at math, but is not a strong speller.

@ Somebody is great at playing the trombone, but he is not a great singer.

@ Somebody can be great at _____, but they may not be a good

at _____ (fill this in any way you like).

All of the people described above have great talents. The fact that there are some things that they are not good at does not take away from their talents. For example, a great baseball player does not become a bad baseball player just because he can't draw well. In the same way, just because someone can't spell well doesn't mean that she can't do math well, and so on.

What Are Your Strengths?

Let's take a look at your strengths. Begin by listing things that you are "Kind of Good At," and the things that you are "Really Good At."

"Kind of Good At" means that you enjoy it and are getting better and better at it, but you still have a lot to learn about it. "Really Good At" means that you are very good at it and that most other people would agree that you are really good at it. You may even have had special recognition for this talent (for example, trophies, medals, certificates), but that isn't necessary.

Try to write down five of each. It can be anything: sports, music, computer, playing a video game, being a great brother or sister, being great with your pets, making a great peanut butter and jelly sandwich, ANYTHING.

Five Things That I'm "Kind of Good" At:

1. _____

2. _____

3. _____

4. _____

5. _____

Five Things That I'm "Really Good" At:

1. _____

2. _____

3. _____

4. _____

5. _____

Take a look at your lists. It should make you feel proud. Remember that you have these talents, especially during those times when you may feel frustrated or a bit sad. Now, let's figure out ways that you can make the most of these talents.

Making the Most of Your Strengths and Talents

When you're good at something, it can feel good to let it show! There are clubs, competitions, shows, and organized activities for nearly everything. These activities will give you the chance to let others see your talent. While it is not a good idea to brag a lot about your talent, it can feel good to let others see what you can do.

For example, did you know about these?

- In Gloucester, England, they have a yearly festival where contestants roll a big ball of cheese down a hill, chase after it, and see who can get to the bottom first.

- There are "Extreme Ironing" competitions to see who can iron clothes in dangerous places.

- There are championships for pea shooting, playing air guitar, and camel wrestling!

- There is a man in China who is famous for writing with his tears.

- There are competitions for all kinds of things that you and your friends may already be doing, including chess tournaments, spelling bees, video game competitions, battles with fantasy playing cards, and so on.

So, no matter what you do well, there is probably a place for you to show your talent!

To make the most of your talents, don't forget to **practice, practice, and practice**.

Although there may be some stress involved with practicing and competing, you will get a good feeling from doing well at something. That good feeling will help you to deal with all sorts of problems in life!

Finding Strength in Others

It is also important to remember the strength that you have in others! Even though at times, you may feel like you don't have many friends, there are people who care about you and who can make you feel good about yourself. Parents, brothers, sisters, friends, classmates, teachers, counselors, and so on. Yes, you may argue with these people at times, that is only normal. That doesn't mean that you can't go to these people for advice, to share something positive, or to just talk. Write down their names on the following page.

Three People in My Life That I Can Go to for Support:

1. _____

2. _____

3. _____

And remember, not only do you depend on these people sometimes; they also depend on you! Don't be afraid to help others. You can help by talking, offering help, or just by listening. This too will make you feel good about yourself.

Finding Strength in Your Beliefs

People have beliefs that can help them to get through life's difficult times. These beliefs come from our religion, our culture, our family, and our own ideas about life. Don't forget about these beliefs! They are there to help you. They can help you to think about your life in a way that can help you to deal better with stress.

What beliefs are really important to you?

Strong Beliefs That I Have Are (you need to list only one, but you can list more if you like):

_____

_____

_____

How can you remember and practice your beliefs?

- If your beliefs are part of your religion, then there are ways to remember and practice them through your religious practices.

- You can remember your religious beliefs through prayer.

- If you do not have any religious or spiritual practices, you can still find ways to think about, remember, and use your strong beliefs.

- Meditation (remember Chapter 4) is a great way to remember your beliefs. You can focus on a phrase or word that reminds you of these beliefs.

- Some people like to remember their beliefs by saying or thinking about them the same time each day (for example, before they go to bed or when they wake up).

CONCLUSION AND CELEBRATION

If you've completed all or most of this book, you know a lot more about managing stress than you did before. If you have been practicing some of the suggestions, then you are at least a little calmer and more relaxed.

Remember: You can't get rid of stress. There will be times in your life when you may be very frustrated.

But don't ever forget: YOU ARE NOT ALONE!

Everyone feels stress. This is part of life. But it can help an awful lot if you can start to use some of the skills and ideas discussed in this book.

Good luck with your new stress management skills!

Congratulations!

You have now completed your own Stress Management Igloo. You can color or decorate the Igloo any way you wish. You may also want to hang it up somewhere where you can see it every day. This will remind you of all of the skills that you have learned and to keep "cool" when under stress.

Bibliography and Resources

MY STRESS MANAGEMENT IGLOO

Name: _____

Date Completed: _____

Books for Parents, Educators, and Therapists

Chorpita, B. F. (2006). *Modular cognitive-behavioral therapy for childhood anxiety disorders.* New York, NY: Guilford Press.

Dacey, J. S., & Fiore, L. B. (2000). *Your anxious child: How parents and teachers can relieve anxiety in children.* San Francisco, CA: Jossey Bass.

Frank, T., & Frank, K. (2003). *The handbook for helping kids with anxiety and stress.* Chapin, SC: YouthLight.

Sterling-Honig, A. (2009). *Little kids, big worries: Stress-busting tips for early childhood classrooms.* Baltimore, MD: Brookes.

Tummers, M. E. (2011). *Teaching stress management: Activities for children and young adults.* Champaign, IL: Human Kinetics.

Zucker, B. (2008). *Anxiety free kids: An interactive guide for parents and children.* Waco, TX: Prufrock Press.

Books for Children

Belknap, M. (2006). *Stress relief for kids: Taming your dragons.* Duluth, MN: Whole Person Associates.

Dunn-Buron, K. (2006). *When my worries get too big! A relaxation book for kids who live with anxiety.* Shawnee Mission, KS: AAPC Publishing.

Kerstein, L. H. (2008). *My sensory book: Working together to explore sensory issues and the big feelings they can cause.* Shawnee Mission, KS: AAPC Publishing.

MacLean, K. L. (2004). *Peaceful piggy meditation.* Park Ridge, IL: Albert Whitman & Co.

Nemiroff, M., & Annunziata, J. (2011). *Shy spaghetti and excited eggs: A kids menu of feelings.* Washington, DC: Magination Press.

Romaine, T., & Verdick, E. (2005). *Stress can really get on your nerves!* Minneapolis, MN: Free Spirit Publishing.

Therapy Games and CDs

I can relax! A relaxation CD for children. Created by Donna B. Pincus. Available through The Child Anxiety Network, www.childanxiety.net

Indigo dreams. A series of CDs with music and stories designed to help children with stress and anxiety. Created by Lori Lite, Available through www.stressfreekids.com

The self-esteem game. A board game that highlights the value of self-esteem. Available from Child Therapy Toys 1-866-324-7529 or www.childtherapytoys.com

Stop, relax, and think. A board game that includes relaxation, impulse control, and problem-solving strategies, Available from Childswork/ChildsPlay 1-800-962-1141 or www.childswork.com

Think positive game. A board game that teaches positive thinking strategies as applied to problem solving. Available from Childswork/ChildsPlay 1-800-962-1141 or www.childswork.com

Websites

Anxiety Disorders Association of America: www.adaa.org

The Child Anxiety Network: www.childanxiety.net

National Autism Association: www.nationalautismassociation.org

Worrywise Kid *(information and resources on anxiety and stress disorders in children):* www.worrywisekids.org

AAPC PUBLISHING

P.O. Box 23173
Shawnee Mission, Kansas 66283-0173
www.aapcpublishing.net